Poverty U.S.A.

POVERTY
U.S.A.
by
Thomas Gladwin

Little, Brown and Company • Boston • Toronto

To my wife

Contents

Poverty U.S.A.

1

Introduction

SCARCELY three years ago the United States declared War on Poverty. It was to be a civil war, a battle against the poverty only of our own people. With poverty abroad we have been content to skirmish, and to confuse even our skirmishing with talk of other wars, both cold and hot.

The war at home is, in contrast, a real engagement. Not only have great amounts of money and numbers of people been committed, but our President has further committed himself, and therefore us, actually to win the war. Really win, just like a real war, so that poverty will be driven from the United States. This can be dismissed as rhetoric, but for those directing the war it reflects a true intent.

This is a new kind of war in the history of the world. Even utopians, while talking of a society free from want, regularly devise schemes which include continued care for the needy. Yet now the President

1

of the most powerful nation in history has declared that no one in his country shall be poor. He has backed his promise with an array of major administrative innovations and commitments. Like landing a man on the moon, overnight a fantasy men dream about has become a concrete national goal with special agencies, program plans, facilities, budgets, and all the other appurtenances of a routine government operation.

Will it work? Can the war if adequately funded really be won? Can poverty cease to exist, even if in only one country? The cynics and conservatives say no, and muster traditional but compelling arguments to bolster their pessimism. Others, idealists if you will, insist it must be won. The War on Poverty, they say, brings to a crescendo a theme of compassion and concern of man for his fellow man, and of big government for little people, which had its beginnings in the New Deal. If this war is lost perhaps the whole pulse of social reform which has beaten strongly and steadily for a third of a century since 1933 will falter, and so-called laissez-faire economics will once again come to reflect the true image and values of America.

Thus far the signs are not encouraging. Solid achievements have been few, and those poor people who have been encouraged to find their voices have spoken out in complaint and disillusionment. They are saying in rising chorus that despite the sound and fury nothing has really changed at all in the slums and in the sharecroppers' shacks except their own expectations and hopes, and that these hopes are being frustrated as fast as they grow.

Have we already lost the war? Certainly it is too soon to tell. But perhaps it is not too soon to begin asking whether we are waging the war as well as we can, with appropriate strategies. We have had some experience by now, both good and bad. Perhaps more valuable, we have a long perspective of past experience against which to measure present performance. The crucial past history, of course, was of the New Deal. As we shall see, the contrasts and comparisons it offers with the War on Poverty are extraordinarily rich and suggestive. But the history of poverty does not begin in the 1930's.

Mankind was born to poverty. We can be sure that the first man, whatever his posture or the size of his head, had little he could call his own to help him in shaping his destiny or even in staying alive. Since then the resources man commands have grown to such size and variety that we in Europe and the United States now genuinely wonder how to avoid being drowned in our own affluence.

Not so, however, the rest of the world. From a world perspective poverty still seems man's condition, with our own riches an exception affecting only a favored minority tucked away in the northern hemisphere. Otherwise, except for Japan and areas essentially European in population such as Australia, the statistics of poverty are all too familiar around the world. They include millions of dying babies, hundreds of millions of people deteriorating from undernourishment, and most of the world's people looking to a future in which their very survival seems to rest not in their hands but with a fickle climate, a greedy landlord, or a self-serving bureaucracy. The gulf, furthermore, between the rich nations and the poor is growing ever wider because poor countries lack the resources with which to grow richer at a fast enough rate. For much the same reasons, within most poor countries the gap between the few people who are rich and the many who are poor is also growing.

Indeed our own earlier history in Western Europe and America shows a similarly tiny privileged class living apart from masses of very poor people. The Industrial Revolution, while extending affluence from the privileged few into a newly enfranchised middle class, consumed in its cruel factories poor people by the thousands.

It was not until the latter half of the nineteenth century that social theorists first began to speculate about a possible world in which there no longer need be masses of people consigned at birth to lives of poverty. However, this was to remain for many years

4

a radical, if not downright utopian, conception. More conventional thinkers argued the economic necessity of a large supply of unskilled (and therefore un-privileged) labor. Surprisingly, one still hears insis-tence upon the need in any society for a *lumpen-proletariat,* although the obvious changes wrought by automation have forced the proponents of this view to add to their purely economic rationale more subtle psychological justifications.

The first third of the twentieth century saw the United States embark upon a period of unparalleled growth in both capital assets and productivity. It was during these years that we first entered on a genuine economy of abundance. True, control of this abundance remained concentrated in the hands of a relative few, among whom the most successful were later to be castigated by Franklin Roosevelt as "eco-nomic royalists." Social justice still came only for those cast in the Horatio Alger mold. Yet these were the years in which the foundations were laid for an economy potentially so productive that true social justice could at last be talked about as if it were realistically attainable. Nor should it be forgotten that in the middle of this period, which we tend to associate with unbridled profit taking, the first major legislation was enacted designed to redistribute wealth from those who have it to those who do not. This was the graduated income tax, a piece of legislation which was bitterly fought not merely for what it did, but, with true foresight, for the precedents it set.

This era was the final heyday of the unbridled right of private personal property. The right to control what one owned and to use it to one's own advantage had been unquestioned ever since mercantilism and the Industrial Revolution overwhelmed the feudal lord obligated to his serfs. Even Karl Marx was caught up with the idea of property ownership. The only way for the proletariat to receive the proper fruits of their labors in his view was for them to control through ownership the means of production. It is interesting that Samuel Gompers had a far clearer perception of the future when he insisted that capitalists should retain ownership of the means of production, but that they should be forced in bargaining with strong unions to share the fruits of production with the men who are the producers.

The event which symbolically closed this era a third of the way into the twentieth century was one which is being repeated all too often today. It was a spontaneous and anguished dramatization of the hurt caused by a system no longer in harmony with the needs of the people it controlled. This event was the Bonus March on Washington, a prototype for the riots which now sear our urban ghettos. The Bonus

Marchers of 1932 were unemployed, starving, desperate. In their desperation they turned to their government and said in effect: "We are decent people who are willing to work for an honest wage. We are caught in a system which offers us no jobs. It is not our fault, yet our families are starving. We have served our country in the past. Our country must now serve us." The fact that the Bonus Marchers were veterans undoubtedly contributed to their feeling that they had a right to speak out. Their message, however, was echoed by many thousands more who were not veterans but were unemployed and starving.

What we now call the "power structure" was bewildered and shaken by the Bonus March, even though they responded in now familiar fashion by calling out the troops and routing the demonstrators in pathetic disarray. It was absurd and unreasonable they said for people to demand jobs when it was quite clear that there were no jobs available. Yet in a humane sense the marchers' complaint seemed justified. How then were these two conflicting views, each essentially just, to be reconciled? Their reconciliation provided the central theme of the New Deal which was to follow.

2

The New Deal: The First War on Poverty

THE NEW DEAL in time met the demands of the Bonus Marchers and created jobs for people eager to work where no jobs existed before. What does this mean? It means that a lot of new programs and economic principles became a lasting part of the American scene. But it means more than this. It means too that basic changes had to take place in our system of values; our responsibilities came to be ordered by a new set of priorities.

The businessmen who had no jobs for the Bonus Marchers and their thousands of unemployed fellows did not put forward the argument that they had no money with which to pay additional wages. Instead they said business conditions were bad, they could not make a profit if they hired more people, and it was not *their* responsibility to risk a loss in order to give jobs to other people, no matter how deserving.

They were in effect appealing to — or indeed taking for granted — the primacy of the right of private property and their own exclusive right to the benefits of their own property, a principle deeply rooted in the Judeo-Christian ethic.

Another pervasive value, however, also holds a central place in the same ethical system, and in addition receives particular emphasis in the documents with which the Founding Fathers launched the United States. This is the right to equality of opportunity. This promises in effect that anyone willing to strive toward a goal has a right to compete equally with anyone else. It is this right upon which the Bonus Marchers were insisting. They were willing to work and work hard. Why then should the opportunity to work be denied to *them* when others no more deserving than they were still being employed? Faced by the human distress which followed from an insistence upon the primacy of private property, the New Deal had as its essential achievement a downgrading of its priority. Through a variety of mechanisms it became clearly established in law and in custom that equality of opportunity was a right more to be respected even than private property.*

* However, any change in values as sweeping as this requires more than the single generation which has thus far passed before it can be complete. Exactly this same conflict between the right of private property and equality of opportunity is at the heart of the current strife and debate over open housing.

A third value must also be mentioned. This value did not play a central role in guiding the programs in the New Deal, but it needs to be articulated precisely for this reason. It is of special significance because it essentially defines the task which the New Deal left undone. It affirms the dignity and worth which adheres to every individual simply because he is a human being. It too is a major theme stressed by the Declaration of Independence and other key documents in our history and of course appears with special prominence in Christian teachings. In part, but only in part, it says that the right to enter into competition for the privileges and benefits which our society offers must not be denied to anyone because of the color of his skin or any other personal quality. The programs of the New Deal were not discriminatory on the basis of race, religion, or any other stigmata, but they did not insist upon nondiscrimination with anything approaching the determination of current administrations. However, there is more to the concept of individual worth than just nondiscrimination. Nondiscrimination after all is only a special case of equalizing opportunity to compete for a goal. A belief in the worthiness of all people demands more. It demands that we value and support even those who do not try to compete. It means that everyone gets something: those who win the race, those who lose, and even those who do not enter the race at all. The New Deal helped both the winners and the losers, but the point to note here is that it virtually ignored the bystanders.

Within the terms familiar to us today the central goal of the New Deal was to guarantee not merely a fair break but, as far as possible, a decent way of life for anyone willing to strive, to delay gratification, and to do the other things we now identify as middle-class behaviors. Nowadays among social reformers it is fashionable to look upon the middle class with something close to scorn and to emphasize its smugness and conformity and selfishness. The world of the 1930's, however, was very different from the 1960's. People even though they espoused middle-class values and attitudes had little reason in those days to be smug. It is easy to be smug in one's virtue in an era when virtue pays off. In the Depression the middle-class virtues did not buy groceries. The man who was willing to work hard and conform found himself as helpless as any loafer to support his family or to discover steps which would lead him along a path of hope for a better future. Furthermore, there were millions of people caught in this trap, ashamed, confused, desperate. In sheer numerical terms they presented the central social problem of the decade and thus commanded the highest priority.

It was not only the anguish and the numbers of the unemployed but psychologically "middle class" poor of the 1930's which determined they should have priority in social action under the New Deal. Perhaps more important was the fact that no intellectual or moral foundation had yet been laid for offering real help to people who were not prepared to help themselves. True, there was in our heritage the parable of the prodigal son, but also there were the wise and foolish virgins. The reinterpretation of Christian ethics under Calvinism and the Protestant Reformation had long since determined which parable would provide the better model. Only those who were willing to work were fit to be saved, in heaven and on earth. Chronically poor people were called paupers or bums, or more likely were just ignored. They were, in the words of Alfred P. Doolittle in Shaw's *Pygmalion,* the "undeserving poor."

However, in the years which followed, novelists like Steinbeck, anthropologists like Oscar Lewis, and sociologists like Michael Harrington, with many others to follow, drew a new and more sympathetic portrait of the chronically poor. This new picture showed people caught in a vicious trap of circumstance, a way of life in which one learned not to care and often discovered that sacrifice and struggle just made things worse. The literature which grew around this new conception of poverty was a tender mixture of brutality and compassion. It showed people struggling pathetically against hopeless odds, but yet hoping, usually in vain, that where they were crushed their children would somehow be spared.

At first, in the 1940's and 1950's, the response to a wakening appreciation of the insidious effects of what came to be known as the "culture of poverty" fell still in the traditional mold of relieving its consequences or symptoms. Social agencies referred to "multi-problem families" and sought devices through which their workers could reach the very poor, not realizing that it was not their agencies which controlled the sources of hurt in their ill-served clients. Finally, largely because of the enlightenment which came first from the civil rights movement, it became clear that the very poor not only did not have the power to fight their way out of the trap they were in, but were actually trapped by a system in which other people were using *their* power, intentionally or not, to keep the poor where they were. Ironically, as often as not the people exercising this power were the very ones who had themselves been ransomed earlier by the New Deal. Thus a whole generation of very poor people, including large numbers of Negroes, grew to their maturity and on to a premature old age largely untouched by the reforms of the New Deal and frequently ineligible for its benefits. The War on Poverty of the 1960's came into being as a war to rescue these hostages left over from the 1930's, and to build a more secure future for their children and their children's children.

The New Deal programs found expression in a multiplicity of laws and of agencies, many of them new. Washington came to be known as "alphabet soup" from the initials of its many agencies: AAA, NLRB, WPA, CCC, PWA, SEC, PHA and on and on. Each agency had its own policies, its own battles, and its own constituents. Yet standing back now with the perspective of the years which have passed it is possible to discern the broad general strategies which found partial expression in each program. It was the repeated and consistent application of these strategies at many points in the social and economic structure of our nation over a span of several years which made possible those massive and permanent changes in our way of life and our value systems which constitute the heritage of the New Deal.

The problems of the 1930's were particular to that era and the strategies for coping with them had correspondingly to be tailored to the times. They would in many respects not be appropriate to the problems and the circumstances of the 1960's. No one has suggested that we repeat the error of which our military planners are constantly accused of trying to fight current wars with the strategies and weapons which proved victorious in the past. Nevertheless in the broadest sense the challenge facing the

War on Poverty is comparable to that of the New Deal. The strategies required to achieve the ends envisioned for each of these campaigns are at least threefold: first, changes in deep-seated attitudes and values held by society at large; second, new expectations and behaviors and skills to be learned by the poor whose life styles are at issue; and third, extensive alterations in the economic and political structure such that newly opened avenues of opportunity will remain open in the future. These are not limited goals. They imply sweeping reforms which add up to what anthropologists would call directed culture change. As in any major alteration in a complex culture no person or social institution remains unaffected by the ripples (or shudders) which run outward from the central impact. The question therefore is not what specific strategies can be transferred bodily from the New Deal to the War on Poverty. Rather our task is to look back upon the New Deal to see what we can learn from this experience which will once again guide us in the awesome but little understood process of directed culture change.

Three broad lines of strategy can be discerned running through the tapestry of programs which collectively constituted the New Deal. Each was focused on one of the critical ingredients of change noted above: changing social attitudes toward the poor, enhancing the capabilities of the poor, and changing the political and economic structure to assure that the effects of the New Deal would endure. These strategies can for simplicity be referred to as *witness, social competence,* and *structural change.*

By *witness* is meant the constant repetition throughout the land of new kinds of transactions and relationships between the government and its people and between man and fellow man.* To assure that the American society and its economy would find a place for every person who was ready to come forth and be recognized meant that doors of all kinds had not only to be opened but kept open. Applicants for programs had to be welcomed when they felt like showing up, not solely when they had been summoned by a higher authority.

President Roosevelt found that people were frightened and demeaned when they discovered

---

* Used in this way "witness" at once evokes an association with Christian evangelism. Without the intention of affirming or denying a basis in Christian ethics for either the New Deal or the War on Poverty, it can nevertheless be observed that both these political programs share at least one strategic necessity with evangelism. This is the need to persuade people to adopt new values, and at the same time new ways of behaving which will be in conformity with those values. One way of teaching these new behaviors is by offering repeated examples of people actually acting in deliberate response to the new values. It is this particular strategy of persuasion which was first given explicit recognition in the context to which the term "witness" is here applied.

their society had no place for them. He therefore exhorted them to put away their fear, and then commanded that a place be found for them. Every alphabet soup agency of the New Deal was required to welcome all comers with dignity and to invest them with responsibility. They were to do this furthermore in every city and every hamlet of the country. In a time of fear and despair the sheer pervasiveness of the New Deal agencies was reassuring and carried with it a new sense of purpose. Everywhere there was someone who cared and had the means with which to give substance to his concern. Thus, although in one sense the National Recovery Administration could be said to have failed because the Blue Eagle which was its symbol was shot down by the Supreme Court, before this happened that same Blue Eagle and the magic letters "NRA" had shone forth reassuringly from literally millions of store fronts and other agencies and enterprises across the country. Simultaneously the large corporations, large unions, other organizations of all kinds, and state and local governments were being exhorted and badgered and legislated into compliance with the thesis that they had a larger obligation to both their employees and their clients than simply to run a taut ship and show a profit.

The result of all this was electric. It was impossible long to remain unaware that times had

changed, and apparently changed permanently. Almost overnight the Bonus March looked in retrospect
like a bad dream. It became hard to understand how
the plea of the marchers for jobs could have gone so
callously unheard. Despite the cries of "leaf raking"
and similar labels which are always attached to any
program of relief, working for the WPA over a
period of time gained a substantial degree of respectability. In fact, some of the most creative contribu-
tors to the postwar flowering of American culture are
people who can look back proudly to their years in
the WPA. Although there were those who grumbled
about "that man in the White House" to the very
end, there is no question that the efforts of the New
Deal to bear witness to the new obligations of the
Federal Government toward its citizens, and to require that the people who held wealth and power in
the country share in these obligations, were overwhelmingly and lastingly successful.

The same strategy of witness is now a key element
in the War on Poverty. However, it differs significantly in at least two respects from the comparable
activities typical of the New Deal. In the first place
the New Deal's programs of social and economic
reform, built principally around employment opportunity, stood more or less alone on the national
scene. Innovative policies of government agencies
could thus be safely assumed to be in response —

and in witness — to the thrust of the New Deal. In contrast, the War on Poverty as often as not operates in the shadow of the civil rights movement and it is therefore not always clear to which of these two sets of values a given set is in witness. Not only are civil rights programs likely to be more dramatic and turbulent, but above all it is a movement in which every proponent, whether willingly or because he has been coerced by new laws, is inherently a witness for the new justice. This intertwining of the issues of poverty and civil rights is pervasive in its effects, and will be a matter of major concern in the chapters to follow. Suffice it to say here that one result has been to obscure the workings of the strategy of witness as it is specifically focused on poverty.

This comes out for example in demonstrations organized around such poverty issues as lack of jobs, inadequate housing, and other economic burdens of the poor. Although the participants in these demonstrations are usually both white and black and the issues are principally economic, the leaders of the demonstrations are with rare exceptions people whose primary identification is with civil rights. Thus in the public mind and indeed often in the minds of the demonstrators themselves, the goals become associated with civil rights and not the War on Poverty.

Nevertheless, it is perhaps in the public response to these demonstrations, and even to riots, that the effectiveness of the strategy of witness, coupled with explanation and exhortation from the President, shows forth most clearly. Despite the destructive anarchy of riots, despite the threatening demands of demonstrators, and despite large scale involvement in both of persons deviant in appearance and behavior, the response by both press and public agencies time and again is to take very seriously the complaints of rioters and demonstrators that their concern truly is with the economic and political burdens of inadequate housing and slum landlords, of discriminatory justice and police brutality toward all poor minorities, and of unequal availability of economic and social resources of all types. This is their message and it is consistently echoed in the mass media. By now our society is prepared at least to listen. Demonstrations and outbreaks are deplored and skillfully "cooled," but in their wake in most cases come new "concessions," sometimes mere tokens but sometimes real reforms. True, these reforms are seldom sweeping, and because they are usually effected on an ad hoc basis by those with the power and inclination to make immediate concessions they do not often fall into place in a larger grand design of social reform. But this is not the point. The grand design will be implemented by

20

other mechanisms. The point is that acceptance by the public and by significant persons in the community of the complaints of the poor has borne witness once again to the fact that the poor have a right to be heard. It bears witness to the fact that even though they may have beards and police records and speak ungrammatical English (or Spanish) they are nevertheless human beings, their plight is seldom of their own choice or making, and the larger society has a responsibility and obligation to admit the truth of their complaints and do something about the conditions from which these complaints arise.

The change in values which this response symbolizes is a major change. It is a major bridgehead already won in the War on Poverty, an accomplishment which must at least in part be attributed to the strategy of witness. Nevertheless it would be a mistake to conclude from this and from the analogous use of the strategy of witness under the New Deal that we can expect that the rolling ground swell of support which President Roosevelt enjoyed throughout the 1930's will underpin President Johnson and his War on Poverty in the 1960's. There are a number of reasons why this is so, but probably most important is the background of the people who are the targets of our current campaigns.

This is the second major respect in which the strategy of witness is different now from that of the

New Deal. The poor whom the New Deal undertook to help were middle class in their orientation. Once they had been put on their feet they were ready immediately to go forward on their own and to assume a responsible place in the community. No one needed to tell them of the need to register to vote and they had no difficulty in seeing the relationship between the Roosevelt Administration and its policies on the one hand and the upward turn in their own fortunes on the other. Not only that but because of the nearly universal desolation spread by the Depression, the number of people whom the New Deal helped to lift by their bootstraps represented a very significant proportion of our total population. The result was that millions of people were prepared to testify and witness for the new ideals fostered by the New Deal. Thus the Roosevelt Administration in effect generated its own witnesses, its own electorate and its own mandate as it went along.

In contrast the target population of the War on Poverty comprises a smaller constituency. Even if it were to form a coherent electorate in support of the Johnson Administration it would not have nearly the power of the New Deal's mandate. Furthermore, despite the articulateness of their leaders the cultural deprivation which characterizes the poor of the 1960's produces a very limited understanding of cause-and-effect relationships in the larger world and thus an inability to see clearly a relationship between voting and major social reform. Add to this a spate of other political issues currently affecting the poor — civil rights, education, and the draft to name a few — which divide the leadership itself, and inevitably people who at best understand the political process only dimly are themselves confused and divided by a multitude of promptings.

It is in fact extraordinary in view of the political liabilities which encumber the War on Poverty that so much has been accomplished. Not only is it largely unable to generate an effective electorate as it goes along, but it also generates built-in resistance. The reforms demanded have required sacrifices and created genuine anxieties among powerful people who until recently saw no need to change their way of doing business. Considering this combination of circumstances the wellsprings of the legislative support, especially in 1965, for the War on Poverty become something of a mystery, perhaps even a miracle. When we add to this a recognition that its essential justification, especially by President Johnson, rests almost entirely on moral grounds it is hard to avoid a small lump in the throat and a realization that the American democratic process sometimes rises to rather notable heights. If nothing else this compels those concerned with devising social strategies to search urgently for sufficient wisdom to meet an extraordinary opportunity and responsibility.

A second but less important strategy of the New Deal was directed toward enhancing the *social competence* of people. By this is meant the capability of a person to participate effectively in those legitimate activities of his society which are open to him. The elements of social competence of course include specific occupational skills, but they also embrace a more general ability to get along in the world of work, of family, of consumers as well as producers, and of citizenship. The socially competent person is the one who is "making it" and is reasonably comfortable doing so. The strategy of social competence then consists in developing programs which will equip people who want to improve their lot, but who for one reason or another are not making it, to develop the abilities necessary for fulfillment of a satisfying social and occupational role. For this strategy to be effective there must be available, first, a supply of people motivated but lacking the skills necessary to move themselves upward; second, a technique or procedure which will effectively provide the essential skills; and third, positions in the occupational or social system which will be open to them once they are qualified.

Under the New Deal the strategy of social competence held an important place but it was secondary to the other major strategies. The reason for this was very simple. The people the New Deal was trying to help were principally those for whom the pathways to employment and opportunity were closed not so much by their own lack of social or occupational readiness as by a straightforward lack of jobs. Yet the Civilian Conservation Corps, a number of youth programs, and some programs of the WPA added up to a significant expenditure of effort directed toward implementing the strategy of social competence, particularly by developing psychological and technical readiness for employment. Thus the New Deal did not hesitate whenever necessary to train people narrowly or broadly as the needs of particular programs dictated. However, the majority of persons who benefited from the New Deal were those who were already prepared to take hold of almost any opportunity presented to them. The big need was seen to be for opening up opportunities.

The present War on Poverty stands in striking contrast to the New Deal in the priorities assigned to programs of training for social competence. The bulk of the funds allocated to the Office of Economic Opportunity and its sister agencies is committed to training objectives, with programs ranging all the way from the preschool world of Head Start, through the Neighborhood Youth Corps and Job Corps of adolescence, and on into the variety of less clearly structured adult programs including the training of indigenous nonprofessionals.

The reason for this emphasis on development of social and occupational skills is readily apparent. The whole conception of the War on Poverty rests upon a definition of poverty as a way of life. The intellectual climate in which it was nurtured was created by studies of the culture of poverty, notably those of Oscar Lewis in Mexico City. This research appeared at about the same time that a spate of studies were published on juvenile delinquency in American slums. Together they demonstrated that certain characteristic life styles emerge in grudging response to the poverty of the slums in almost any large city. This life style is acquired by children and stays with them throughout their lives. Although it presumably provides a basis for survival in a slum, it can readily be shown that many of its attributes are distinctly inappropriate and maladaptive when transferred to other more fortunate settings. Many more studies are now available, they have been extended to Appalachia and to other rural areas and to other countries, and research interest is beginning to focus on the secondary differences rather than on the major similarities between one area and the next. However, the uniformities remain striking and have therefore provided the basis for programs at the national level designed very explicitly to correct the social, occupational and psychological deficits of people born and raised to a life of poverty.

The question of the effectiveness and the strengths and weaknesses of the social competence strategy must be deferred until we examine the War on Poverty as such. However, an implication of the heavy reliance upon this strategy should be made explicit in order to round out the contrast between contemporary priorities and the philosophy and premises of the New Deal. It implies in effect that the culture of poverty is so pervasive and ramified that there is no step-by-step way to improve one's circumstances within it. Instead it is necessary to be trained for an entirely new role, to make a clean break, and to move out freed of the shackles of the earlier environment. The point at which one shifts onto a different track varies of course with the program. The premise upon which Project Head Start was launched for example was that once an adequately prepared child enters school he will be able to keep up with the middle-class children all the way through and thus ideally at least be prepared to step into a middle-class role as soon as his schooling is completed. To take another example, the indigenous nonprofessional once he has completed his training is said explicitly to be embarking upon a "new career," leaving behind the old — although in this case his work often will carry him back to his old environment from which he will in turn help others move out of their predicament.

The difference in emphasis on social competence in the New Deal and the War on Poverty reflects a difference in the way the problem of poverty was defined for each. The New Deal said in effect that social and economic systems need only be changed in such a way as to open up more employment opportunities. Most people would then be able to move directly into them without additional help and their problems would be solved. The view now in the 1960's is that the part of the social system in which the remaining poor find themselves is so inherently damaging that no amount of tinkering will solve the problem. The principal hope for them is therefore seen to rest in developing sufficient strength and skill to maneuver themselves, largely by their own efforts, out of where they are and into something better. Corollary to this is the belief that if any reforms are feasible in the existing social system these will have to be accomplished through vesting poor people with the political and administrative power necessary to force the changes *they* consider important upon the power structure.

The New Deal, in contrast, did not systematically invite advice and suggestions from its beneficiaries, did not encourage them to organize in public protest (except for strikes), and with the exception of consumer cooperatives (largely rural) did not try to give them direct control over the programs under which they were benefited.

Reforms instead were instituted almost entirely from above and were achieved through *structural change*, the final key strategy of the New Deal. This consisted in altering, principally through federal legislation, the distribution of income and money within the United States, and inevitably through this means reallocating power, both directly and indirectly. A number of these interventions consisted in the introduction of new mechanisms which, although they appeared relatively simple, struck so directly at the heart of major economic structures and relationships that their net impact was vast, almost incalculable. One of these, for example, was the creation of the National Labor Relations Board. Although this was ostensibly set up as an agency to regularize the relationships between labor and management, the regulations which it administered and the authority which it was granted had the effect of redressing overnight a balance of power in labor-management relations which had in the past overwhelmingly favored management. In fact the balance seems by now to have shifted so far that the unions, assured of their power, now look more and more like charter members of the conservative establishment and have largely lost the spark of real reform. In any event the change was sweeping and its effects penetrated to every corner of our economy and into many of our social institutions. All of this took place without making any appreciable changes in the input or outgo of federal revenues.

In contrast to the NLRB most of the New Deal agencies reallocated power largely by reallocating money, often but not always through payments to and from the Federal Treasury. Here one thinks first of the Social Security Administration. It established programs which take money from employers as well as employees and reserve it for later return to the employees. The still growing Social Security program, coupled with pension funds and other benefits won through collective bargaining under the NLRB, not only serves to take money from capital and give it directly or indirectly to labor, but has also re-affirmed the responsibility in our society of employers for the larger welfare, not merely the working conditions, of their employees.

Another pervasive change was wrought in a different sector of our economy by establishment through the Agriculture Adjustment Act of an intricate series of price supports, crop controls and other regulations. These programs, which of course persist in modified form to this day, have interesting ethical implications relevant to the debates presently swirling around the concept of a guaranteed minimum income. The dilemma of the small independent farmer of the 1930's was in several important respects similar to that of the unemployable poor slum dweller of the 1960's. Both were people whose skills were no longer needed, at least in the numbers in which they were available. Although in both cases there were often secondary factors involved (drought and the Depression in the 1930's and discriminatory hiring in the 1960's) both populations were disadvantaged by technological advances which permitted large operators to achieve high productivity per man hour through the introduction of technological improvements financed by heavy capital investment. As a result the small farmer could not survive on the money he could get for his crop and the poor person who comes to the city looking for a job cannot survive on the money he can get for his labor. A key difference, however, distinguishes these two groups of people on the basis of how they are perceived and stereotyped by the larger society. The poor slum dweller is usually black, or Spanish-speaking, but in any event is tagged with Mr. Doolittle's label of the "undeserving poor." In contrast the small farmer and his farm are enshrined by the mystique of our pioneer heritage as the cradle and repository of the cherished American qualities of independence and integrity. Of course, as John Steinbeck eloquently documented in *The Grapes of*

31

Wrath, when these small farmers found themselves
displaced and economically useless they soon
adopted behaviors which earned them an entirely
new stereotype as "underserving" Oakies.

Nevertheless the majority of the small farmers
clung tenaciously to the only way of life they knew
and stayed on their farms just as people nowadays
remain in the urban ghettos because they know no
other place to go. The response of the Roosevelt
Administration to their impossible situation was a
program of subsidies and price controls whose cost
to the present day in both direct payments and in
elevated prices paid by consumers is almost incalculable. The Federal Government in effect through its
agricultural policies has determined to support indefinitely the small farmers of the United States even
though their contribution is in many cases even less
necessary to the economy than is that of the unskilled laborer whose income it is now proposed
should also be supplemented. Although the analogy
of price supports for the farmer to a guaranteed
income for a poor person cannot be pressed too far it
is important to note that crop controls and other
related aspects of the price support program involve
direct cash payments to farmers, in return for which
they not merely do nothing but in fact have to agree
to desist from the productive work they would otherwise undertake. It seems then that perhaps the moral

issue involved in a guaranteed income is not so much a matter of paying people enough to live on even though they do no work as it is a matter of how one defines people as worthy of such payment.

Returning to the New Deal, still other mechanisms can be cited. The Rural Electrification Administration and the Tennessee Valley Authority were bold efforts to check migration from country to city. The Securities and Exchange Commission gave the little investor rights and protections which have undoubtedly contributed importantly to the historically new phenomenon of the wage earner-capitalist. Without extending the list further these are sufficient to underscore the fact that the New Deal relied heavily on the use of legislation and new federal mechanisms to introduce a whole series of revolutionary structural changes in the allocation of power and the ability of one class of people to exert influence on another in the United States.

It is not surprising that structural changes of this sort occupied a major place in the New Deal. Although they required a good deal of daring the disaster of the Depression was so great that almost anything seemed better than leaving things as they were. Furthermore, starting with the stock market crash of 1929, the Great Depression of the 1930's unfolded as a progressive collapse of all of our intricately related economic institutions. The system broke down and the people caught within it were helpless to save themselves. It therefore seemed logical that the principal changes had to be made in the structure of this system and not in the people. Once it had been modified and strengthened the individual would again find a productive place for himself within it. Thus were developed the characteristic priorities of the New Deal: major reliance on structural change, supported and sanctioned as necessary by the strategy of witness, with social competency low on the list. This last was based on the assumption that the reservoir of social competence in the population at large was already adequate and needed only to be sustained long enough for the system again to accommodate a backlog of people ready to go to work.

In contrast the War on Poverty has been launched in an era of pervasive affluence. Despite occasional dislocations the vast majority of people see very little wrong with our basic economic structure. Even the threat of automation is beginning to be discounted and question is raised whether someone was not crying wolf. Under these circumstances it would at best be difficult to justify major structural changes and reallocations of power within our economy. Add to this that poverty is viewed nowadays more as a disabling way of life than as unbalanced income distribution and it should not come as a surprise that

34

the current emphasis is on people and the development of their social competence rather than on structural change.

Yet it is widely agreed that in another area our society does suffer from a seriously unbalanced distribution of power and that major corrective changes are urgently needed. This is of course the area of race relations and the gross inequality of power between white and black. Federal civil rights legislation and the programs launched by this legislation have therefore relied heavily upon the introduction of precisely those kinds of structural changes in the allocation of power which are left out of the War on Poverty.

The prior enactment of these often disturbing structural reforms in the name of civil rights undoubtedly served as a further barrier to the introduction of structural changes designed to deal specifically with poverty. It is as if we had spent ourselves in a flurry of reform and had used up our capacity to change the system any more. Yet the irony of this historical sequence is already becoming apparent. Despite a great deal of legislation, carefully designed and often demonstrably effective in reducing discrimination, the vast majority of Negro families, as well as Mexican-Americans, Puerto Ricans, Indians and others are little if at all better off than they were a few years ago. They are still very poor, too poor often to take advantage of their new rights. Civil rights leaders themselves are now articulating with increasing urgency the need for money and jobs, and the goal of integration has become secondary and sometimes is even rejected. Thus the reform movement of civil rights now finds that its success hinges upon the success of the reforms of the poverty program, and yet the latter seems to lack the power to effect the changes necessary to keep the momentum of the whole enterprise moving.

3

War Is an Extension of Politics

An ASSESSMENT of the present circumstances and future prospects of the War on Poverty must begin by taking into account certain broad constraints and conditions which history and politics have introduced. Together they put definite limits on the range of strategic alternatives available. First, it is a war in which the initiatives rest principally with the Federal Government. Second, it was declared at the height of another domestic war, for civil rights, and the two remain inextricably intertwined. Finally, its principal political and moral justification rests on a conception of poverty as a way of life from which people solely by their own efforts cannot escape, and which is therefore not their own fault. These three factors each reinforce the other and together account for much of the developmental history of the War on Poverty to date. These are the realities within which we must work.* It is therefore worth reviewing briefly their origins and implications before moving on to look at the elements of poverty and the alternatives available to cope with them.

The indigent poor have not always been a responsibility of government at any level, certainly not of the Federal Government. Traditionally they have been cared for by private charities. From the 1930's onward the Federal Government assumed increasing leadership in developing Social Security and welfare programs for the poor, but these were intended principally to sustain the incapacitated and indigent so that they would not starve. The helping hand which would lift people out of poverty, or at least make their lives more meaningful, remained vested in community agencies, usually privately supported. The community agencies, staffed principally by social workers, for years conveyed the impression (especially during fund raising drives) that their clients were actually being rehabilitated and thus removed from the welfare rolls. However, when

* It might be added that the War on Poverty came into being in the context of yet another war, in Viet Nam. These wars are related insofar as they compete for resources from the same reservoirs, but the war in Viet Nam is not otherwise relevant to our discussion here. Our discussion presumes that resources will remain available at some meaningful level for deployment in the War on Poverty, but it can do nothing to contribute toward assuring the continuance of these domestic programs if other priorities prevail.

actual studies were undertaken it became increasingly clear that this was not so. The poor were staying poor. In reaction to this disillusionment, when the Office of Economic Opportunity came into being as the strategic headquarters for the War on Poverty it set out to take the initiative not merely away from traditional social agencies but also from social work as a profession. After some historic battles not only within local jurisdictions but notably also with the Department of Health, Education, and Welfare this posture of OEO was substantially compromised. Nevertheless, the principle remains that a strong federal initiative provides an essential counterbalance to stultifying traditionalism.

Another reason for centralizing the direction of the War on Poverty at the federal level was the expectation that many of its innovations would be revolutionary. They would consequently be resisted by those villains of our latter-day social melodramas collectively known as the "power structure," or more elegantly as "the establishment." Only at the federal level, it was argued, would there be sufficient strength and commitment to persevere against the stratagems of local political and financial interests. This concept of a federal-local confrontation was carried so far that some of the language in Title II of the Economic Opportunity Act seems almost to provide for federal support for organized insurrection against local authority. In a few cases the OEO has in fact been accused of precisely that. These accusations were accompanied by strident outcries of protest on both sides, outcries often quite out of proportion to the threat which local organizations of the poor could possibly pose to local power groups. Nevertheless this points up a paradox which repeatedly besets almost every one of our current efforts at social reform — civil rights, poverty, and the broader range of programs identified with the Great Society. In 1964 the American people elected a President and a Congress largely committed to revolutionary social interventions. Then after vesting their government with this power they turned around and as individuals massively resisted the programs which were enacted. This has been especially true with respect to civil rights, but it also is evident in the poverty program as well as others. Whatever the reason for this peculiarity of the American governmental process in the mid-1960's, it is by now generally agreed that any program potentially as revolutionary as the War on Poverty must find its principal support and direction at the federal level. Consequently, the alternatives to be considered in the chapters which follow will in the main be predicated upon federal initiative and power.

It is probably no accident that the War on Poverty was launched at a time when the country was at a peak of activity and concern over civil rights, but their coincidence was by no means an unmixed blessing for the former. The attention focused by civil rights programs on the plight of the Negro in the United States forced the American public to recognize openly for the first time that the vast majority of Negroes live in abject poverty and that there is no way for them to escape its chains. Without this new realization it is probable that the War on Poverty would never have come into being. Yet the historical fact that the poverty program was in a real sense born out of the civil rights ferment has resulted in such ambiguity and confusion that its consequences could in the long run prove disastrous. One set of problems and issues surround civil rights. Another set are operative with respect to the problems of the poor. There is a lot of overlap between them, but there is also much which is distinctive to each. However, poverty and civil rights have become so intertwined not only in the public mind but also in the professional literature that poverty is often taken to be essentially a Negro problem. True, almost every article dealing with the matter points out that the majority of persons falling below almost any arbitrarily determined poverty income level are *not* Negro. Yet these same authors usually appear satisfied with a single disclaimer and make relatively little effort thereafter to separate in their analyses the effects of being poor from the effects of being black.

The inclination to lump these two factors together is readily understandable quite aside from the historical origins of the civil rights and the poverty programs. Subjectively it is almost impossible for a Negro living in the slums to distinguish his poorness from his blackness. Also, the continuous delineation by civil rights leaders of the problem of Negroes in terms of inadequate job opportunities, housing, health care, and so on, gives more prominence to the problems of poverty among Negroes than among other populations with less articulate spokesmen. Furthermore, the fact that these lacks are stated often with anger and indignation in a context of racial discrimination implies that all of the economic disadvantages from which Negroes suffer are a consequence of discrimination and the conscious withholding of economic resources from Negroes by those who control these resources. Regardless of the truth of this view, its constant reiteration has the effect of deflecting attention away from the working of purely economic forces operating in the marketplace and affecting *anyone* who is poor. This can be a particularly serious handicap because purely economic factors, as we learned in the New Deal, are often much more amenable to change than are prejudice and discrimination.

The confounding of civil rights and poverty has thus had several distracting and probably harmful effects. A lot of issues have been lumped together, confusing the planning of programs by making it difficult analytically to distinguish separate causes, effects and alternative solutions. Attention has been deflected away from the surprisingly large variety of non-Negro populations who live in poverty, and who actually outnumber Negroes in the poverty category. Finally, the poverty program itself has been caught up in the political issues which surround civil rights, many of which have generated for OEO even more hostility and resistance than any of its own programs would attract in their own right.

The third constraint on the War on Poverty arises from its moral justification. It was pointed out in the preceding chapter that the people for whose benefit the War on Poverty is principally being waged are those least likely to exert initiative in helping themselves. They respond to adversity with anxiety, withdrawal and resignation. Although we are prepared to extend a helping hand to a person no matter how often he fails as long as he keeps on trying, as the beneficiaries of the New Deal were wont to do, our Calvinist tradition inclines us to reject as undeserving those who do not try. This has meant that a special rationale had to be developed to make the War on Poverty morally and politically acceptable. The rationale was found in a formulation which asserts that the victims of poverty are rendered by the conditions of their life incapable of responding constructively to the challenges of the world about them. These analyses take the form either of describing a vicious circle of cause and effect or else the more amorphous concept of a culture, a life style, or a ghetto which surrounds and shapes the individual along avenues of self-defeating behavior. It is obvious that, regardless of its undeniable accuracy and its effectiveness in overcoming our scruples against helping people who will not help themselves, a formulation of this sort seems also to define the condition of poverty as one so enveloping and ramified as almost to defy solution. Instead of pointing to a series of interventions each of which can be expected to have a modest but measurable and cumulative effect, it seems to say that nothing short of a radical reshaping of the total situation or else total removal of an individual from his environment will have any lasting result.

Each of these two alternatives has actually found expression in a major strategic theme in the War on Poverty. Two principal mechanisms have been developed to meet the first alternative, introducing radical alterations into the life circumstances of the poor. One has been to offer poor people a voice in the decisions regarding programs which will affect them. This is seen in the policy of "maximum feasible participation" of the poor in the decision-making process. In practice it has resulted in efforts to seat on the policy-making body of each major poverty program people who will in some fashion qualify as "poor." Because of confusion between poverty and civil rights programs this has often had the paradoxical result that essentially middle-class Negroes are brought forward to play this role. The other mechanism is the organization of poor people at the grass roots level to develop and exert pressure for lasting reforms. Here again the civil rights issue is often more visible than a concern with poverty as such. Taken together these efforts to increase the power of the poor have given to the War on Poverty much of its distinctive stamp and also have embroiled it in a disproportionate number of controversies. However, we shall later have reason to question how much genuine reform we can expect to achieve as long as we place primary reliance on these two mechanisms.

The other strategy which emerges in response to the concept of poverty as a vicious circle or a way of life is to remove people from this environment. In the poverty programs implementation of this strategy has taken the form of providing people with the necessary training and experience, and sometimes initial employment, to remove them from the ranks of the poor. This is the strategy of social competence referred to in the preceding chapter. It is the one to which the War on Poverty has made its heaviest commitment. For its success it depends not only on effective training programs, which are in fact being brought into being in increasing numbers, but also on permanent job opportunities with at least minimum career potential being available at the time training is completed. The difficulty seems to be that training programs must either be so sweeping in their results that an almost Pygmalion-like transformation takes place, or else the occupational structure must provide a growing number of openings for precisely the kinds of minimally skilled people whom labor economists say are being squeezed out of the job market by automation and related phenomena. In other words, this alternative seems to require sweeping and revolutionary changes in our society, yet it does not incorporate mechanisms for achieving the necessary revolution.

Thus we see that the particular historical circumstances which surrounded the War on Poverty at its birth carried with them several implications which may have compromised the overall effort more seriously than was at first evident. These developments were probably inevitable given the constraints under which the War on Poverty initially developed, but they are not necessarily irreversible. If the experience of these initial exploratory programs can be capitalized on now and transmuted into new strategies which are more truly effective the efforts of the first years will have been well worth all their frustrations.

Once again we must remind ourselves that poverty has been with mankind since the beginning of time. It will not be eradicated even in one rich country without a great deal of experimentation into all sorts of tactics, not all of which will be uniformly successful. This seems to be a time of pause, of rethinking and of regrouping, in the War on Poverty. A number of critiques are appearing and new strategies are continually being proposed. The chapters which follow are intended as a sympathetic and hopefully positive contribution to this reappraisal.

4

Poverty Is Being Poor

ONE OF the more extraordinary characteristics not
only of the War on Poverty itself but also of the great
amount currently being written about poverty in
general is the relatively minor attention which is being given to the immediate and direct consequences
of simply being poor. Being poor has a large number
of secondary consequences such as powerlessness, inadequate access to resources, lack of education, and
a poor diet. However, these follow and are derived
from a primary condition of just being poor. Being
poor, at least in the United States, consists in a lack
of sufficient money to function effectively in the
economic system through which everyone is forced to
seek the necessities of life. Let us examine what this
means for day-to-day living.

Having at any one time at most only a small
amount of money, and never being sure that in the
immediate future enough will be available to cover

48

even minimum needs, the poor person is forced to spend whatever he has on the most urgent demands which arise each day, and thus to operate constantly through a succession of very small deals. Instead of a weekly trip in the car to a supermarket, food must be bought by walking to a neighborhood store and buying only enough for the next meal or two. The size and the adequacy of the purchase, and therefore of the meal to follow, depends on how much money can be scraped together on that particular day. Improvident, inefficient? Of course. But to do otherwise calls at least for a car, a reserve supply of money, and reliable refrigeration. Louise Richards in a recent article reexamined the standard guidelines which have been customarily recommended ever since Depression days for efficient handling of household finances: spend first for necessities and last for luxuries, buy the best quality of foods for the lowest price, budget carefully and plan purchases in advance and so on.* She then demonstrated that each one of these budgeting rules, although rational and sensible, is in fact difficult or impossible to follow when one works with a very small and uncertain income.

In an eloquent and angry article entitled "Keeping

---

* Louise G. Richards, "Consumer Practices of the Poor," in *Low Income Life Styles*, Lola M. Irelan, ed. (Washington, D.C.: Welfare Administration, 1966), pp. 67–86.

the Poor Poor" Paul Jacobs has described the variety of people and of commercial practices which surround the poor person and take his money.* Although they keep him poor they also provide the only channels open to him for spending the small sums of money which he can command at any one time. Without a car to get to work it is very hard to obtain a decent job (especially in an area without public transportation such as Watts), but without sufficient funds for a substantial down payment the only cars available are nearly worn out. When they break down the necessary expensive repairs will only be performed for cash. The poor person who needs to spend money to meet installments or pay bills cannot sustain a checking account and if he is lucky enough to be working cannot get to a bank or a post office for a money order. Consequently he must purchase a commercial money order at a rate governed only by what the traffic will bear, and of uncertain reliability. Food and other products are often available in the poverty areas at lower prices in less than standard qualities, but once these products are identified as below standard they often can go very far below without intervention of legal or other controls. The manner in which poor people are gouged and exploited by excessive installment payments and carry-

* In *Economic Progress and Social Welfare*, Leonard H. Goodman, ed. (New York: Columbia University Press, 1966), pp. 158–184.

ing charges has become notorious. Mr. Jacobs describes a variety of other less well-known credit arrangements to which the poor are often forced and which in the long run soak up still more of their meager resources.

Mr. Jacobs is profoundly sympathetic toward poor people and their dilemmas. He has several times joined poor people in their daily lives after deliberately divesting himself of all but a pittance of money. Finding himself and his new friends surrounded by people ready to take every penny they have and give very little in return he not surprisingly has become angry. He holds those people who are exploiting the poor responsible for what they are doing and his anger is therefore directed at them. He is also angry with the rest of us who complacently let the exploiters go on about their business. This anger is felt by the poor themselves. It expresses itself among other things in the smashing and looting of stores which is now a standard feature of urban riots. These attacks on local merchants are not merely a means for obtaining otherwise unavailable goods but also rather clearly reflect a smoldering resentment against people who are seen as coming into the slums to prey upon their inhabitants.

Inherent in the angry resentment directed toward shopkeepers, loan agencies, landlords and the like is an assumption that the mechanisms they use to extort money from poor people have been deliberately devised as a way to make large profits and grow rich. Put the other way around it is assumed that if they were willing to make a little less money they could give poor people deals as favorable as those which middle-class people enjoy. As we shall see, this is almost certainly not true.

Not only is exploitation perceived as deliberately contrived to maximize profit, it is also seen by its victims as discriminatory against whatever minority group occupies the slum area involved. It would be surprising if they saw it any other way. Members of minority groups in cities are constantly faced with insulting reminders of their inferior status and therefore inferior rights and privileges. It is thus only natural that they should also interpret the economic policies which they encounter as deliberately designed further to disadvantage them *because* they are Negro or Puerto Rican or Mexican-American or whatever. In addition, the car dealers and money lenders and landlords are more often than not English-speaking whites. As a consequence when there are riots not only are the stores of white merchants the principal targets for vandalism, but business enterprises run by members of the local ethnic group can usually escape damage simply by advertising prominently the ethnic affiliation of the proprietor. This is true even though in many cases the actual business practices of these establishments differ little if at all from those practiced by whites.

Undoubtedly ethnic discrimination contributes to the development of the commercial practices which so disadvantage poor people. It is hard to imagine white middle-class customers putting up with the usurious rates, shabby merchandise and run-down facilities which poor Negroes, Puerto Ricans and Mexican-Americans usually accept without audible protest.

Beyond this, however, two much broader economic principles are at work, principles which must almost inevitably apply to any really poor people regardless of their color or speech or culture. The first and most crucial of these principles constitutes a central tenet of all commercial transactions in any free economy: the larger the deal the better the terms. At the upper end of the scale stands the man about whom we so often hear who can get it for you wholesale. However, attention is very seldom focused on the other end of the scale where the principle inevitably becomes the converse: *the smaller the deal the worse the terms.* Costs which tend to accrue at a fairly fixed level per deal or unit of business, costs such as handling, packaging, negotiating, carrying inventories, paying rent and so forth, and the less tangible costs reflected in making judgments and accepting risks, all these costs are proportionately lower when a large number or high value of units are involved in each deal. Conversely, when these factors are all added into the cost of completing a very small deal this cost necessarily becomes highly inflated. Even riding a bus costs more when tokens must be bought one at a time to conserve cash. A larger markup is needed to pay the rent, the overhead and the wages of a full-time clerk in a neighborhood store whose daily volume is usually very small.* In other kinds of transactions the size of the deal can become sufficiently small that entirely new bases for making profits must come into play. Despite the very high interest rates which are charged on small loans to poor people the risks are so high that it is not possible to make a profit from interest payments alone. The profit margin is therefore deliberately planned to come from the equities in repossessed merchandise which a succession of defaulting borrowers are forced to surrender. In other cases dishonest practices, like putting a thumb on the scale, become so widespread among retailers trying to assure their own living that they are almost

* The cost of doing business is often further increased for the small shopkeeper by the unwillingness of large wholesalers to deal in his small orders. He has to buy at necessarily higher cost from local jobbers who serve his kind of store. Some slower moving items, especially perishables, he even buys one or two at a time from the supermarket or other large retail outlet and then resells at an additional markup. (Elliot Liebow, personal communication.)

taken for granted. At least they are accepted by poor people without protest, perhaps because protest would be in vain. But accepted or not these practices further rob the poor person of his rights, his money, and his dignity.

The high cost of doing business through a series of very small deals applies to anyone and is an inherent attribute of the economy of poverty. Unless there is some way to make the deals bigger or else to reduce the risk and high costs involved in transacting business with people who have practically no money, it is hard to see how even the most kindly of businessmen could support themselves in a poor neighborhood without charging exorbitant rates and prices or offering substandard goods or services or both.

A second major principle almost as crippling for a poor person as the first is the need in many kinds of transactions for substantial financial resources before being able to enter into any kind of deal at all. Sometimes this takes the form of a requirement for actual cash, as in the down payment on an automobile or the deposit required for a telephone. Because they are unable to assemble the necessary amounts of cash at one time, persons who could afford the monthly charges for telephone services or the monthly payments on a fairly good car are often denied these facilities, yet these are facilities critical for effective articulation with the larger commercial world. Both a telephone and a car are essential in applying for and obtaining a job, finding out about and capitalizing on sales and other sources of bargains, or obtaining medical and other services without wasting a good part of a day on them. If it were somehow possible to compute the monthly cost in added expenses and lost income of not having a car and telephone it is probable that this figure would not differ widely from the monthly cost of operating and paying for both.

The resources necessary to get a transaction under way need not take the form of cash. An obvious alternative is to obtain credit at reasonable cost. However, this can usually be achieved only through already having substantial assets that are convertible into cash, or else someone prepared to guarantee repayment of the loan if it is defaulted. Since poor people are very unlikely to have many convertible assets or rich relatives they cannot obtain these guarantees. There is of course another basis for obtaining credit. This is to have a steady and reliable income at a level high enough to pay for necessities with a little left over. Welfare payments are often fairly steady, but are usually at levels so low they do not really cover necessities, much less leave a little over, so they are no help. The only steady income which can leave some extra cash over is a good job, but this is precisely what the poor person almost by definition does not have and usually cannot get. Therefore poor people who have to buy something of some size must either do so on credit at very high interest rates and with the constant threat (and cost) of repossession, get it dishonestly, or else do without. When it comes to essentials, doing without usually means that needs have to be met through alternatives which in the long run are even more costly. Inability to obtain a mortgage frequently results in paying rent at a higher level than mortgage payments, in return for which there is instead of a growing equity only the prospect of a lifetime of shabby accommodations.

Another class of deals which can only be consummated if cash or credit are available in some quantity involves the provision of professional services, especially legal and medical services. Some effort is made to provide both of these for poor people through governmental programs, but they are usually poor in quality, limited in scope and obtained only through the exercise of patience and persistence. Outside of criminal cases, legal services are virtually unavailable to a poor person who, for example, wishes to sue for damages (except in cases of clear liability with a fairly certain outcome) or to recover something which he believes was taken from him by fraud. With respect to health, the miserable and humiliating medical care which poor people must expect is too well known to require comment. Positive and personal medical or legal attention to the problems of a poor person, regardless of his race or language, is usually available only if he is clearly in risk of dying, or is about to go to jail, or has cash.

If, to borrow Paul Jacobs' phrase, the poor are kept poor not simply because of deliberate exploitation and discrimination, but also because being poor is economically so inefficient that people are usually unable to escape from poverty by their own efforts no matter what they do, what does this suggest with respect to planning programs to help poor people? One conclusion which emerges compellingly is that even complete elimination of discrimination against members of any minority group will not substantially improve their life circumstances if they are genuinely poor. Leaving aside questions of personal ability and training, and regardless of the sentimental history of how our Italian or Irish or Jewish ancestors made it from rags to riches, it seems inescapable that if you are born in the mid-twentieth century of really poor parents in an urban slum (or on a sharecropper's farm) the purely economic dice are loaded so heavily against you that the likelihood of your achieving a position of real dignity or security is almost precluded. Put in another way, if only *equal* opportunities are extended to the minority poor and they are therefore subject to the same rules of business which govern middle-class people their limited cash resources will prevent them from deriving any lasting advantage from this "equality." Thus many of the demands which are currently being made by civil rights leaders in northern as well as southern cities appear impossible of fulfillment within our economic system as it presently operates.

The solution furthermore does not seem to lie in trying to coerce businessmen to offer to poor people deals on as favorable terms as they would offer to middle-class customers. The cost both direct and indirect of doing business exclusively in small deals prohibits the offer of terms as good as those which govern large deals without either a subsidy, or else bankruptcy. In other words, regardless of the moral character of businessmen who operate in the slums as bankers or employers or merchants, there is no basis on which they can do business which will simultaneously be fair to them and their customers. At least one has to lose. If this is true it points unequivocally to the need for some new additional factor in the economic life of poor people through which they can at least have a chance to become self-starting along the road toward improving their circumstances. What this new factor should be is probably already evident, because it consists in an already familiar proposal.

Everything which has been said thus far points

strongly in the direction others have been pointing with increasing urgency over the past several years. This is toward the adoption of a policy of guaranteeing for everyone some minimum level of income sufficient to assure at least modest decency and security. A number of different ways have been proposed for accomplishing this and all have been analyzed for their relative cost and effectiveness from a variety of points of view.* Although advantages of one sort or another accrue to each of these proposed plans, for our present purposes their relatively minor differences are far less important than the central principle of guaranteed income maintenance.

Formidable problems of administrative policy, political and moral acceptability, and fiscal feasibility must be resolved before a guaranteed income can become a reality. Yet with increasing unanimity people who are looking at the problems of poverty from almost any point of view, whether they are social scientists or economists or blue ribbon advisory commissions, are arriving at the conclusion that a guaranteed income must be a part of the solution. Without it people in our society who are

* Alvin L. Schorr, "Alternatives in Income Maintenance," *Social Work*, 11 (1966), 22–29; Helen O. Nicol, "Guaranteed Income Maintenance: Negative Income Tax Plans," *Welfare in Review*, 4, no. 4 (1966), 1–10.

disfranchised by poverty and discrimination will never achieve full participation in the way of life which is supposed to be the right of every American to enjoy. Various arguments are advanced to support this position. The one set forth here rests upon the relative efficiency of economic transactions as a function of income. To recapitulate in summary form, below a certain level transactions become so small that their nature changes and sinks into rapidly increasing inefficiency. In addition, at this level of income there can be no surplus, hence no savings, no real control over the future and therefore no advantage in trying to plan ahead, and no security. Some means must therefore be found to permit people to stabilize their economic activity at a minimal level of efficiency and predictability. The only way to do this is to see that enough money is regularly available to sustain this level of activity. The guaranteed minimum income is the only mechanism thus far proposed which will effectively meet this requirement.

There has also been considerable discussion of the overall national cost of various income maintenance plans and how this relates to the level of income which should be considered an acceptable minimum. This includes consideration of factors which might offset the direct costs, although among these attention has been largely limited only to potential reductions in existing welfare programs. However, the factor of relative economic efficiency as a function of the size of transactions, which has been reviewed here, would undoubtedly also affect the net program cost. Yet it would be almost impossible to anticipate in any concrete terms the subtle interplay of increased efficiency, decreased uncertainty and risk, and gradual increase in derived benefits such as improved employability, health, and so forth which might result. As in the case of the sweeping economic reforms of the New Deal, the ramifications of something as fundamental as a guaranteeed income program cannot be estimated accurately in advance, and perhaps there is no reason why they should be. Not even the most pessimistic critic has suggested that a plan of this sort would bankrupt the country, nor indeed that it would require allocation of more than a very small percentage of our overall national revenues. If we are truly serious in our commitment to abolish poverty in our country, and if we accept the very compelling evidence that below a certain level of income it is impossible to escape a heritage of debt and insecurity and misery, then we are forced to recognize that without some floor under income the remainder of the program is almost certain to fail, leaving the majority of poor people no better off than they were before. Yet we should also bear in mind that income maintenance alone cannot abolish poverty even though without it no other strategy is likely to succeed either. It is one thing to strike off the chains of poverty, another to develop full financial and social security. Income maintenance can do the first, but not the second.

The argument of this chapter thus far has been couched primarily in economic terms. This is appropriate because the goal of any guaranteed income maintenance program is economic enfranchisement of poor people in the larger world of people who already have sufficient income to be full participants in the economy. Nevertheless we must digress briefly here to consider the possible psychological consequences of a program of this sort. The reason for this is that the argument most commonly advanced against income maintenance is not economic. Instead it is psychological and moralistic. With our thinking shaped by a strong Calvinist tradition we deplore people who live only for the present and take no initiative to help themselves. We see them as a different kind of people from ourselves and doubt their ability ever to learn or even aspire to what we would consider our upright attributes. The conclusion from this line of reasoning is that once poor people have assurance of a minimal but sufficient income for the rest of their lives without their having to work for it, great numbers of them will be delighted to sink permanently into a life of idleness and leisure.

What will actually happen? There is of course no way to predict with certainty the outcome of any program which is designed to alter radically the life conditions of large numbers of people. However, it is worth noting at the outset that what poor people themselves are asking for, not merely through their articulate leaders but also when they talk to reporters who interview them on corners, and when they scrawl slogans on walls during demonstrations, are jobs and an end to exploitation. They are not demanding something for nothing. As a matter of fact the idea of a guaranteed income has thus far evoked very little response from leaders who have risen from the ranks of the poor. Furthermore, although it is difficult to document, whenever an actual choice is presented between obtaining money by working for it and obtaining it as a dole, even the poorest people appear to select the avenue of work.

The difficulty is that the choice under present conditions, and particularly under existing welfare policies, is seldom equal. Under the eligibility rules governing most welfare programs, even the most modest support payments cease as soon as a person is employed. Although the minimum income from a job may be greater than the welfare payments, and almost certainly is not less, the kind of jobs open to poor people generally offer far less security than does welfare. Furthermore, a person who has gone off welfare to take a job then must suffer delays and go through complicated procedures and indignities before being reinstated. For someone upon whom others depend and who is without savings to fall back upon this uncertainty can represent a frightening hazard. Under these circumstances taking a job may represent an uncertain choice. It is precisely for this reason that all of the various income maintenance plans thus far proposed incorporate mechanisms designed to assure a constant minimum level of support which will not be jeopardized by employment or discrimination.

Middle-class anticipations of the effects of a guaranteed income are all too often based upon one or two examples known at first hand. Middle-class people, however, have only limited contacts with poor people and the only ones they know are often domestic servants, usually women employed by the day or week, to do cleaning, cooking and baby-sitting. Every now and then one of these women stops working, planning to live instead on an income derived from welfare or Social Security. The employer is scandalized and the stereotype of the shiftless dependent poor person is once again confirmed. The situation, however, is seldom seen from the standpoint of the woman who has quit her job. Leaving aside the fact that she probably has been treated with condescension and otherwise finds domestic employment psychologically somewhat humiliating, her tenure in the job is insecure and her employment is likely also to be suspended without pay any time the family by whom she is employed takes a trip or a vacation. The woman usually has some children at home and if she does not receive her pay the children have less to eat or may even be evicted. Domestic employment furthermore usually requires that a person be in the employer's home at a time when the employer as a wife and mother needs help the most. Especially if she is a Negro, the maid probably lives in poor housing downtown and has a long bus ride to and from the home of her employer in the suburbs. This necessarily results in the employee, probably also a mother and a wife, being forced to deny to her own family the very care she is being paid to give to another woman's family. In stereotyped middle-class terms she can choose between on the one hand being a self-respecting member of the labor force but an irresponsible mother, or on the other hand being a good mother but accepting welfare "handouts." It cannot be denied that under these circumstances the introduction of an income maintenance program would probably result in further substantial defections from the ranks of domestic service. Although this should not objectively be taken as a demonstration of anything except the ability even of poor people to make rational choices, it will in fact doubtless be seen as evidence supporting the stereotype of the irresponsible poor. Since the more influential people are also those most likely to employ domestic servants, the sheer inconvenience of losing household help may alas prove to be a significant factor in determining the future of such a program.

Lacking solid evidence upon which to base predictions of the behavior of poor people once they are assured of a guaranteed income one is forced to fall back upon the negative argument. It possesses, however, a rather compelling logic of its own. Put in simplest terms the argument is that as long as poor people are caught in a trap compounded of lack of money, uncertain employment and welfare programs which penalize initiative, it is inevitable that the majority will surrender to these overwhelming odds and give up the unequal struggle to rise from their lives of misery; therefore if we want them to live in a fashion we would consider more upright an essential first step is to relieve those pressures which exist to keep them in their present condition. To reject this argument amounts almost to saying that the poor are beyond hope and incapable of helping themselves under any conditions. To accept the argument requires only a faith that most human beings will, like ourselves, try their best with what they have, provided they see some reason to hope that their efforts might be productive.

We can now turn to the second broad principle

which blocks effective participation of the poor in our economic system. This is the requirement that for many transactions involving both goods and services the purchaser have available either credit or a substantial amount of cash before the transaction can be initiated. Examples have already been cited, including the purchase of automobiles and housing and the obtaining of services ranging all the way from a lawyer to a telephone. It is of course conceivable that under an income maintenance plan the minimum level could be set high enough so that surplus could be accumulated and held in reserve for these purposes. However, this would make the projected cost of a guaranteed income program so high that its enactment in the foreseeable future would be extremely unlikely. Furthermore, since many of these expenses are nonrecurring, raising the minimum level of income would probably not be the most efficient, and certainly would not be the most straightforward, approach to meeting occasional needs for larger sums of cash.

In actuality there is already available at least in rudimentary form a mechanism for meeting these needs. This mechanism is public welfare. Inasmuch as most proposals for guaranteed income maintenance are designed to replace the majority of welfare programs with far simpler administrative procedures, existing staffs of welfare agencies could provide a large pool of trained manpower to implement a reoriented program of special grants, mortgage guarantees, purchase of professional services, and the like.

However, existing welfare policies and the philosophy underlying them would have to be drastically overhauled before welfare agencies could effectively serve these new goals. Ever since the enactment of the Poor Law of 1834 in England public welfare has operated on the premise that all able-bodied and morally upright people should be gainfully employed; any able-bodied person who requires welfare support must therefore have some defect in his character, a defect which should not be encouraged by any reward of money.* Welfare laws have therefore been designed on the basis of an essentially negative philosophy, that of discouraging idleness. If welfare is to be productive it must instead encourage productive lives by providing the security and facilities essential to that end. Instead of supporting disablement, welfare should instead strive for enablement.

Poor Law philosophy has led over the years to development of a veritable thicket of regulations and policies designed to insure that lazy or otherwise "undeserving people" cannot "take advantage" of

* Blanche D. Coll, "Perspectives in Public Welfare: The English Heritage," *Welfare in Review*, 4, no. 3 (1966), 1–12.

welfare programs. It has been estimated that one out of every five welfare dollars is spent simply in policing eligibility under these regulations.* Some of the consequences of these policies have been eloquently summarized by the recent report of the Advisory Council on Public Welfare:

> Public assistance payments are so low and so uneven that the Government is, by its own standards and definitions, a major source of the poverty on which it has declared unconditional war.
>
> Large numbers of those in desperate need, including many children, are excluded even from this level of aid by arbitrary eligibility requirements unrelated to need such as those based on age, family situation, degree of disability, alleged employability, low earnings, unrealistic requirements for family contribution, durational residence requirements, and absence of provisions for emergency assistance.
>
> The methods for determining and redetermining eligibility for assistance and the amount to which the applicant is entitled are, in most States, confusing, onerous, and demeaning for the applicant; complex and time consuming for

* Richard A. Cloward and Frances Fox Piven, "The Weight of the Poor: A Strategy to End Poverty," *The Nation,* May 2, 1966.

the worker; and incompatible with the concept
of assistance as a legal right.*

In addition, as we have already noted, these regulations serve to stifle initiative and often discourage
employment. Furthermore, they require that an uneducated poor person cope with a highly complex set
of administrative procedures which frequently far ex-
ceed his comprehension. It is, incidentally, probably
significant of the kind of thinking which goes into
welfare programming that the solution often proposed by welfare planners for this complexity is not
to simplify programs but rather to designate selected
persons with some title such as "urban agent" to
guide the poor person through the maze, thus piling
yet another service on top of those already existing.
Finally, it is through bureaucracies, both public and
private, governed by these regulations that the role
and status of poor people is principally defined in the
larger society. Yet welfare agencies and welfare
workers do not wish to be tarred with the same brush
as the clients they represent. Consequently they
establish additional policies and definitions which

* *Having the Power, We Have the Duty,* Report of the Advisory
Council on Public Welfare to the Secretary of Health, Education,
and Welfare (Washington, D.C.: Government Printing Office,
1966), p. xii. For a more personalized account, see Richard M.
Elman, *The Poorhouse State: The American Way of Life on Public
Assistance* (New York: Pantheon, 1966).

will assure that the poor keep their distance and have an identity distinct from the agency and from the middle-class public which supports this agency.*

Even this brief and incomplete summary of the criticisms which are leveled at welfare programs is sufficient to suggest the magnitude of the overall job which will have to be done before welfare agencies can respond effectively to a new philosophy and a new challenge. In the first place, before public welfare can serve a new and enabling role in conjunction with an income maintenance program all of the old concepts of eligibility must be swept aside. Eligibility for income maintenance has been conceived, in all of the plans proposed, in simple and straightforward terms with the assumption that once established it would not thereafter be subject to continuous question and reexamination. The same policy should apply also to welfare assistance.

Secondly, the kind of help principally offered by welfare programs must change from diffuse minimal support to individually tailored and focused help in obtaining the more exceptional goals and services not included in day-to-day expenses. Welfare can, in other words, meet the need for cash or its equivalent for down payments, deposits, and the like. This bears

* Gideon Sjoberg, Richard A. Brymer, and Buford Farris, "Bureaucracy and the Lower Class," *Sociology and Social Research*, 50 (1966), 325–337.

some similarity to the special grants which are occasionally and grudgingly made by welfare agencies to buy a refrigerator or stove. However, for many kinds of purchases guaranteed low interest loans would probably serve as well or better than cash grants. As we have noted earlier, in many cases relatively modest assistance of this sort can be expected to result in substantial increases in earning capacity and reduction in expenses of many kinds ranging from the costs of illness to junked or repossessed automobiles. Increases in earning power will permit not only the repayment of loans but also a reduction in the income supplements required to meet the guaranteed minimum. Thus the two programs will supplement and support each other. While loans and grants increase earning power and thus reduce income maintenance needs, the fact that income is guaranteed at a sufficient level will take much of the risk out of credit purchases and reduce their cost and rate of defaults. Professional services, medical, legal and educational, can be supported either by loans or by direct grants or even provision of services.

Welfare programs of this sort for the poor would thus take a form patterned after a familiar prototype, but with somewhat different beneficiaries. This is the program of GI benefits offered to servicemen initially at the end of World War II and continued in more modest form following subsequent wars. Under the

GI Bill eligibility was acquired simply through having worn a uniform within set time limits. It did not matter whether a person had been in combat or not or whether his record was distinguished or mediocre provided only his discharge was honorable. Furthermore, once established, his eligibility was unquestioned unless he was found guilty of deliberate fraud or other malfeasance. He did not have to show that either his character or his mind were improving as a result of the benefits he was receiving; he had only to pay his debts when they were due and obtain passing grades if he was in school. In return he obtained an education or specialized training, support for his family when required, and medical care, insurance, and other services. He also could receive a loan to start a business or buy equipment, or have his mortgage guaranteed when he bought a house, and in general could expect help of all sorts in order to get him started on the road to self-sufficiency and security for himself and his family. For thousands of men who came out of the Army unemployed, unskilled, often uneducated, and frequently thoroughly disoriented the GI Bill provided not only a promise for the future but a program of help and enablement offered with dignity and simplicity. A very high proportion of GI's participated in some or all of these programs and went on to enjoy careers which have been both satisfying and productive. Americans need

74

only to be persuaded that poor people are as deserving as veterans for a similar miracle to be brought about in the world of poverty.

These then are some of the economic implications of the War on Poverty. Although for the poor person not having enough money is only one aspect of a larger experience of humiliation, intimidation and misery, and any total assault on poverty should take all aspects into account, hopefully this chapter has demonstrated that it is important for analytic and strategic purposes to isolate the purely economic element in order to examine its consequences and to explore its possible solutions.

5

Poverty Is Being Despised

IF ECONOMICS is first in importance among the varied forces which combine to keep the poor poor, certainly discrimination is second. Discrimination rests upon negative expectations, upon unfavorable stereotypes, or in a word, upon prejudice. Because the Negro civil rights movement has so strongly protested discrimination we are inclined to think principally of prejudice as affecting Negroes. Yet it applies with equally devastating effect to practically all poor people. In this chapter we will therefore consider both the causes and effects of discrimination, and also the circumstances which have linked this so particularly to Negroes.

Poverty is often described as a vicious circle. Perhaps we should instead speak of a whole succession of circles, almost all vicious. One such is the circle of cause and effect in which being poor means living in a poor neighborhood, which means going to a second-rate school, which means having an inadequate education, which means having a low-paying job or no job at all, and thus being poor. Or being poor means eating poor food and living in unsanitary housing which means having poor health, which means missing a lot of work or school, or perhaps being handicapped or not strong enough to handle the heavy manual work which is often the only kind available, and thus being unemployed much of the time, and so being poor. Being poor also means realizing that most of the other people in the world are more successful and are able to do things about which the poor person can scarcely even dream, which means that the poor person sees himself as a failure, which means he has no confidence and gives up easily or perhaps does not push himself at all, and thus stays poor forever.

All of these circles begin and end with being poor. There are many more like them, each freighted with more misery than the last. Because these sequences of cause and effect seem to repeat themselves endlessly generation after generation the life of poverty is sometimes described as a culture, or more precisely a subculture, with an implication of a self-contained and self-perpetuating cultural dynamic. Furthermore, because a large proportion of the total number of poor people are black an additional refinement of this construct has evolved, namely the concept of a specifically Negro culture of poverty. The concept of a culture, of a way of life associated with a class or category of people, is fraught with a number of hazards. Not least among these is the fact that prejudice must be based upon a presumed set of attributes characteristic of the people being discriminated against. The idea of a culture, in this case a Negro culture, provides a neat pseudo-scientific package of attributes against which to erect a barrier of discrimination. In this context attention has been directed especially at the Negro family and its breakdown. The assumption of self-perpetuation in Negro culture is given particular impetus by efforts to trace the history of the Negro family back to the days when slaves were treated as breeding stock on plantations.

There is, however, an essential inconsistency, indeed incompatibility, in phrasing the life of poverty simultaneously in terms of circles of circumstance touching all the raw nerves of the real world of today and yet also in terms of historical cycles endlessly repeating themselves oblivious to any but the most deliberate intervention. Elliot Liebow has eloquently captured the essence of these contrasting formulations as they are experienced by poor streetcorner men and their families.

Whether the world of the lower-class Negro should be seen as a distinctive subculture or as an integral part of the larger society (at the bottom of it, perhaps, but as much a part of it as those in the middle or on top) is much more than an academic question and has important consequences for "intervention." Marriage among lower-class Negroes, for example, has been described as "serial monogamy," a pattern in which the woman of childbearing age has a succession of mates during her procreative years. The label "serial monogamy" clearly has a cultural referent, deriving as it does from the traditional nomenclature used to designate culturally distinctive patterns of marriage, such as polygyny, polyandry, monogamy, and so on. "Serial monogamy," then, as against the unqualified monogamy of American society at large, refers to and *is used as evidence for* the cultural separateness and distinctiveness of the urban, lower-class Negro.

. . . . .

. . . What is challenged here is not that the marriage pattern among urban low-income Negroes does not involve a "succession of mates" but the implication that this succession of mates constitutes prima facie evidence for the cultural distinctiveness of those to whom it is attributed.

. . . From this perspective, the streetcorner man does not appear as a carrier of an independent cultural tradition. His behavior appears not so much as a way of realizing the distinctive goals and values of his own subculture, or of conforming to its models, but rather as his way of trying to achieve many of the goals and values of the larger society, of failing to do this, and of concealing his failure from others and from himself as best he can.

If, in the course of concealing his failure, or of concealing his fear of even trying, he pretends — through the device of public fictions — that he did not want these things in the first place and claims that he has all along been responding to a different set of rules and prizes, we do not do him or ourselves any good by accepting this claim at face value.

Such a frame of reference, I believe, can bring into clearer focus the practical points of leverage for social change in this area. We do not have to see the problem in terms of breaking into a puncture proof circle, of trying to change values, of disrupting the lines of communication between parents and child so that parents cannot make children in their own image, thereby transmitting their culture inexorably, ad infinitum. No doubt, each generation does provide role models for each succeeding one. Of much greater importance for the possibilities of change, however, is the fact that many similarities between the lower-class Negro father and son (or mother and daughter) do not result from "cultural transmission" but from the fact that the son goes out and independently experiences the same failures, in the same areas, and for much the same reasons as his father. What appears as a dynamic, self-sustaining cultural process is, in part at least, a relatively simple piece of social machinery which turns out, in rather mechanical fashion, independently produced look-alikes. The problem is how to change the conditions which, by guaranteeing failure, cause the son to be made in the image of the father.

Taking this viewpoint does not reduce the magnitude of the problem but does serve to place it in the more tractable context of economics, politics and social welfare. It suggests that poverty is, indeed, a proper target in the attempt to bring lower-class Negroes "into the mainstream of American life," and it supports the long line of social scientists, from E. Franklin Frazier and Gunnar Myrdal down through Kenneth Clark and Richard Cloward, in seeing the inability of the Negro man to earn a living and support his family as the central fact of lower-class Negro life. If there is to be a change in this way of life, this central fact must be changed; the Negro man, along with everyone else, must be given the skills to earn a living and an opportunity to put these skills to work.*

Dr. Liebow's goal of defining the problem in a tractable form is identical with the purpose of the essays in this book. Only through these means can one cut through the mystique of a culture of poverty and isolate for examination each of the multiple causes of discrimination and deprivation. Yet his account, simply by virtue of adding to the already voluminous literature on the Negro family, unintentionally sustains the Negro facet of the mystique, and therefore also sustains one basis for discrimination against Negroes. In fact, however, just as we saw that being poor is not exclusively a Negro problem so also prejudice does not claim only Negro victims. The exclusion, stereotyping, degrading nicknames and insulting jokes which form the cutting edge of discrimination may be most familiar in the case of the Negro, but many other ethnic groups suffer almost equally disabling humiliation. This can only be fully sensed by traveling around the country and listening to people in the Dakotas talking about Indians, in Los Angeles talking about Mexicans, in

* Elliot Liebow, *Tally's Corner: A Study of Negro Streetcorner Men* (Boston: Little, Brown, 1967).

Dallas about East Texans, in New York about Puerto Ricans, in Ohio about Appalachians or even in Hawaii about Samoans. Always there is the same combination of slightly scornful humor built around a stereotype of people who are on the one hand irresponsible and lazy (perhaps charmingly, perhaps not), but withal on the other hand somewhat unaccountable and disquieting in a clannish sort of a way. Always, too, they are poor.

Their poverty in fact is all that unites these various groups who are otherwise very different from one another in color, language, religion and culture. It is obvious that poverty and discrimination are closely and complexly interrelated. For example, putting the relationship the other way around, it is hard to think of any large group of really poor people about whom stereotypes and prejudice have *not* developed. When in the 1930's numbers of small independent farmers, in other times idealized as staunch repositories of the American pioneering spirit, were stripped of their farms and their money they became almost overnight the most stigmatized population of the Depression years, the Oakies. Similarly, the purest descendants of the early waves of White Anglo-Saxon Protestant migration have now become in their poverty the Appalachian hillbillies, probably as ruthlessly plundered of their property and power as any of our minorities except the decimated Indians, and the butts of a special school of American belittling humor which extends back over several generations. The little child in eastern Kentucky, hiding and peeking out in wide-eyed fright at the stranger, knows as well as any child in an urban ghetto that he is powerless to protect himself against a world which has judged him worthless. Under these circumstances what good would it do him to be told that he is a blond, blue-eyed Anglo-Saxon and therefore potentially heir to all the privileges of the land?

The fact that the larger society, impinging upon each of its disadvantaged ethnic minorities, tends to treat them all in similar ways underscores, but also generalizes, Liebow's observation that what we are really seeing is the way our national culture molds the lives of the poor people within it. Not only do members of minority groups find the range of behavioral choices which are open to them severely limited by the forces of discrimination, but they also respond, as Liebow has pointed out in the case of Negroes, in more subtle psychological ways which are again strikingly similar from one minority population to the next.

Time and again one is depressed and ashamed to find that ethnic minorities have accepted and internalized the stereotypes of themselves offered by the dominant majority, stereotypes uniformly inferior and degrading. It is hard to persuade any Negro that there is anything good about being black, and Negroes even taunt and insult each other with the hateful epithet "nigger." Indians will readily tell you that they and their fellows are overly dependent, selfish, and will not cooperate for the common good. Mexican-Americans are convinced they are all dumb because they cannot speak English. Yet Puerto Ricans in New York, often despising themselves, nevertheless make it a point to speak Spanish in public lest they be mistaken for even more despised Negroes, thus denying themselves opportunities to practice the English without which they can never hope to move out of the ghetto.

Correspondingly, insofar as there is a positive side to the ethnic stereotype its victims will cling to a measure of residual pride. Proprietors of stores near Indian reservations may describe their customers as irresponsible drunkards, but in the back of their minds they perhaps remember reading about Hiawatha and they certainly know what happened to General Custer, and so do their customers. Some Indians, too, especially in the Southwest, still have a culture of their own in which they can take pride even if they may no longer themselves participate fully in its values. Similarly, Mexicans have a history of wars (including those with the United States) nobly fought and a country which holds a commanding place in the world. Puerto Ricans can look back upon a Spanish heritage, and Hawaiians upon recent royalty. Only Negroes, despite Black Muslims, Black Power and efforts in Africa to accentuate the positive in Negritude, usually find tragically little in which to take pride.

For each of these minorities there is also an explanation of some sort of the origin of their plight, an explanation which goes beyond simple discrimination to account for both their low status and the inadequacies they are forced to believe are part of their nature. Needless to say not all minority group members accept these explanations equally uncritically. Nevertheless each has surprisingly wide currency. For Negroes it is the history of slavery, the plantation, and the destruction of the family, which formed a deliberate part of this sordid phase in American history. For Indians it is a long history of dependency upon a fickle federal government which, through its treaties and its Bureau of Indian Affairs, is seen as giving with one hand and taking away with the other, forcing the Indian into servile dependency in his effort to get what he can and hold on to it. Mexicans feel themselves indentured in the serf-like relationships under which most of them were originally brought as agricultural workers north to the United States, and further constrained by their lack of English. Paradoxically, while Puerto Ricans ac-

tively differentiate themselves from Negroes in New
York (and even from Mexicans in Chicago, on the
grounds that Puerto Rico gives them a U.S. origin)
Mexicans in the Southwest often voice envy of
Negroes because they can speak English. They also
in their despair believe that Negroes are in more
privileged status than they as a result of civil rights
programs. Puerto Ricans in their turn blame the
meager achievements of their island culture, where
they have lived always in a shadow, first of colonial
powers and then of more aggressive and powerful
Americans from the mainland.

Even the potential leaders from minority groups
seem, with regrettably few exceptions, to turn away
in contempt once they have succeeded in rising out
of the demeaning grip of poverty. Successful Indians,
perhaps feeling guilt because they have not shared
their good fortune as fully as their culture demands
with all of their kinsmen, are inclined to be especially vehement in suggesting that if their fellow
Indians were not so lazy and irresponsible they too
could rise to a better condition, implying that one
needs only the sterling character of the speaker to
surmount the handicap of being an Indian. Negroes
when they prosper usually either detach themselves
completely from responsibility for their fellows and
pursue their own careers or else become self-desig-
nated spokesmen for a community which behind

their backs calls them Uncle Toms, with all the prejudice and selfishness which this implies. Mexicans and Puerto Ricans may, like Negroes (and most whites as well), just mind their own business when they have become successful, but in both Spanish-speaking groups there are also some individuals who, reaching back into their Hispanic antecedents, become *patrones* and, like feudal lords, command loyalty from those they protect and sponsor. These varied responses to success are generally reasonable and understandable, but they result in common in a minimal contribution to the welfare of those who have been left behind. Thus the minority groups which our society has isolated and stigmatized often do not even have the advantage of a leadership which will mobilize and unite them for their common good. Instead they remain divided among themselves and resentful of the fortunate few who have succeeded. Even the civil rights movement has only been able to mobilize enough leaders to work directly with a very small proportion of Negroes.

It would be an obvious oversimplification to suggest that the many commonalities in the way minorities are treated and in the way they in turn respond results solely from their being poor. Nevertheless the only two broad characteristics which mark off all of these people from the rest of society are their poverty and the fact that they are discriminated against. Since poverty and discrimination thus tend to occur together regardless of the color or culture of the people involved it obviously behooves us to look more closely at the relationships between these two forces.

Adaptation to the reality of being poor necessarily calls for a distinctive set of behaviors and ways of handling human relationships. With not enough money to meet daily needs, to say nothing of coping with the unexpected, with little or no power to influence the people who own or control the important things in life, and with such a poor education that the workings of the larger world can only be dimly understood and must therefore always carry the threat of strange and unknowable power, under all these circumstances it makes no sense to plan ahead for a future one cannot control, to save for tomorrow a pleasure or a dollar which someone may snatch away from you tonight, or to leave on someone's shelf something of value which will never be yours unless you take it. Under these circumstances, too, a poor person is unlikely to develop the habits of thrift, honesty, self-discipline, conscientiousness or initiative which an employer values in a good employee or a worker looks for in his co-worker. Almost inevitably, then, a person identified as coming from a background of poverty is little wanted and little trusted in the responsible workaday world. The identification of poverty is furthermore easily made. One need only be poor, not necessarily black or unable to speak good English, to be able to afford only shabby hand-me-down clothes, to smell because there is no bathtub or hot water available, to have bad teeth and weak eyes because of lack of adequate care, or to show up late because the alarm clock is old and broken or the bus is the only available transportation and it is late.

Deprived thus of power or influence the poor person typically must strike out physically to obtain or defend his rights. The middle class in contrast boasts "good manners," which include a multitude of techniques for calming difficult situations, for deflecting anger with words, and for obtaining things by persuasion or purchase. The threat of a poor man's violence is upsetting to a middle-class person not so much for the physical hurt it implies as for the rips it causes in the delicate fabric of relations which bind together middle-class power and security. Add to this the assumption we all seem to make that if we possess something good which we value, another person who cannot also have it will be actively jealous and resentful of our good fortune. Actually, most poor people seem to be so numbed by the hopelessness of their plight that they do not strike back at the fat cats who exploit them but instead deflect their hurt upon themselves and upon their fellows.* Nevertheless the presumption of lower-class jealousy and anger combined with their known habits of physical violence are sufficient to make poor people seem threatening and unpredictable to would-be employers or neighbors or passers-by in the night, regardless of their color. Seemingly the only way to deal with the threat is to keep the poor at a safe distance — in slum ghettos, in jobs for which there is no career bridge into the white collar occupations, and behind the wall erected by social agencies to protect safe and predictable people like "us" from the disturbing turbulence of poverty.

Yet these poor people who make middle-class people so uncomfortable and anxious are actually almost totally powerless. Not only can they do nothing to rectify the broad social injustice under which they suffer, but they are so closely watched they cannot even retaliate effectively against social exclusion and a never-ending succession of personal affronts. Thus, ironically, the barriers of discrimination which we erect against the threat of the poor can only be maintained because poor people in fact lack the power to threaten anyone at all, except perhaps each other.

The poor nevertheless demonstrably belong to the human species. Even in their poverty they are people

* Lee Rainwater, "Crucible of Identity: The Negro Lower Class Family," *Daedalus*, Winter, 1966, pp. 172–216.

just like us. They walk like us, they talk and think more or less like us, perhaps we may admit they even feel like us. Or do they feel like us? This is the crux. We do not like to see ourselves as cruel and insensitive to the feelings of others. Yet if we reject people simply because they have less money than we do this is not right — provided the rejection means the same thing to the poor as it would to us. Therefore we have developed an elaborate rationale which says that everything is really all right because the poor actually feel quite differently than we do. For example, by emphasizing violence and sexuality among poor people we suggest that the poor are a little more like animals than we and therefore must be less sensitive. To this end we make the assumption that poor people not only for some reason enjoy violence but also, like the Natural Man of the nineteenth century, can immerse themselves in sex as an uninhibited expression of their true selves. The evidence actually suggests that the exact opposite is true and that sex in particular, although more talked about, is less enjoyed among poor people than in the middle class.* Nevertheless the stereotype continues to be fostered.

Nowhere is this distorted perception of the morality, sexuality, and worth of the poor more vividly

---

* Lee Rainwater, "Some Aspects of Lower Class Sexual Behavior," *Journal of Social Issues,* 22 (1966), 96–108.

expressed than in current middle-class debates about birth control. More often than not one finds that both the advocates and opponents of expanded programs in family planning for the poor take it for granted that the primary goal is a reduction in the number of children born to poor parents. The argument is of course phrased more euphemistically by its proponents: they say society has an obligation to see that children are not born into a life of misery, as if this were a substitute for doing something about the misery itself. It is understandable that a premise of this sort would be applied to overpopulated and underdeveloped areas of the world, but it is hard to see its moral justification in the United States, the land of plenty. Why, furthermore, should both research and counselling bearing on birth control for the poor focus on their sexual behavior and how to neutralize its procreative effects, instead of assessing the advantages versus the burdens of having children? Middle-class people — affluent, well-organized, rational, and medically sophisticated — not only have no difficulty in paying for and using a variety of contraceptive techniques, but the counselling available to them is in addition invariably couched in terms of the meaning and worth of children and their own role as potential parents. Poor people in contrast are more likely to receive help with birth control, if they do at all, on a production line basis like any other medical treatment or immunization, in effect as a biological rather than a psychological and moral matter. Correspondingly, the degree of success of these programs among poor people is normally judged with respect to their birth rate, not the stability of their families or the mental health of their children. The argument for family planning which is addressed to middle-class people states that through this means they will be enabled to love all their children because they will have only as many as they want. Should it then be otherwise for poor people? Do only their numbers matter? The final turn of the screw is the widespread denial of family planning services to unmarried lower-class women. Thousands of illegitimate children are born to lonely and bewildered young women because of a prudish policy based on a single totally unfounded assumption. Ignoring mounting evidence to the contrary, this assumption posits that the sexual morality of poor people depends significantly upon reasoned decisions regarding the likelihood that conception will result from any given act of sexual intercourse. This assumption is increasingly being questioned with respect even to educated middle-class young people in college. It becomes absurd, if not downright punitive, when applied to poor people whose relative inability to delay gratification has become almost a truism. What is needed instead is development of simpler, more reliable and inexpensive contraceptive procedures, and compassionate counselling in their use.

The stereotype of the unfeeling and less-than-human poor is also found in the popular literature on family life. In the social science literature a number of careful studies are available of the family within different ethnic groups. These consistently underscore the inescapable undermining of family integrity which results from living in poverty: limited choices in choosing a husband or wife, often better occupational opportunities for women than for the man of the family, the combined effects of welfare regulations and of psychological pressures which drive men out of the house, and a general mistrust of other people which poor people acquire in realistic adaptation to a punishing world.* Yet in spite of this evidence the large literature on the family in a culture of poverty, both urban and rural, all too often implies an almost willful irresponsibility and insensitivity, as if lower-class people are incapable of caring about those family values which we claim to cherish.

Although the pioneering scientific work on poverty families was done by Oscar Lewis in Mexico City, the current spate of literature on lower-class family

* Arthur Besner, "Economic Deprivation and Family Patterns," in *Low Income Life Styles*, Lola M. Irelan, ed. (Washington, D.C.: Welfare Administration, 1966), pp. 15–29.

life principally documents Negro family breakdown. Thus once more the poverty problem and the stereotypes which go with it is converted into a Negro problem and laid at the door of Negro culture or, for the more biased, Negro racial psychology. However, it can readily be shown that along with the other characteristics of minority status, the usual statistical indicators of family breakdown — illegitimacy, venereal disease, child neglect, and the like — do not appear only among poor Negroes. Instead they show up wherever income levels are low, whether this is in a Negro or a Puerto Rican slum, or an Indian reservation, or in a Mexican-American neighborhood that does not look like a slum but is.

Why is it that time and again we find the stereotype of poverty is seen as principally black? It obviously cannot reflect reality because even among the total population of poor people in the United States Negroes are a minority. Nor can it be attributed to the fact that most Negroes are poor, because most Indians and Mexican-Americans and even Hawaiians are also poor. It is true that Negroes have far more eloquent spokesmen than any other poor minority group, but this is probably less a cause than a result of an already existing focus on Negroes and Negro problems.

There is of course a long history of concern over the Negro in the United States which has culminated now in the civil rights movement. Parallel to this there is an even longer history of real pressure placed on Negroes, and particularly on the Negro family. Has this special history in fact lent more reality to the stereotypes of poverty as they are applied to Negroes? Undoubtedly both of these historical trends have played some role in the emphasis on black poverty in contrast to all others. Certainly because of this history we became aware first of the plight of Negroes. Only more recently have we noted the similar stresses which result from being a different color of poor.

However, in one respect it must be admitted that the struggle is clearly worse for the Negro than for a member of almost any other ethnic group. The vast majority of Negroes are permanently recognizable throughout their lives as Negroes simply because of their physical appearance. This makes an enormous difference for those who by one means or another have succeeded in lifting themselves out of poverty and are ready to enjoy the fruits of a better world, and then discover that all but a few doors remain closed to them simply because of their color. This is an overwhelming and bitter personal tragedy for anyone to whom it happens.

Yet it is important to recognize that for most Negroes it does not happen. Sadly, they never get that far. In this respect also, then, the majority of

Negroes are little worse off than white Puerto Ricans or Indians or Mexicans who, as long as they all stay poor, suffer almost the same indignities, discomforts and discrimination as do poor Negroes. The matters of color, and of prejudice based on color, which are of paramount importance to more articulate civil rights leaders (who show by their very articulateness their relationship to the rejecting white world) are not issues which necessarily contribute substantially to the day-to-day miseries of a poor Negro in the slum. Naturally any Negro is inevitably aware that he is black and usually equates this blackness with a sense of unworthiness and disadvantage. But so is an Indian aware that he is a "dumb Indian" or the Appalachian mountaineer that he is an ignorant and defenseless hillbilly in a hostile world.

Any poor person living among others like himself carries certain visible stigmata of his status which lead him and others to act in ways which tend to humiliate and disadvantage them. This is a widespread characteristic of poverty, at least in the United States. Quite different is the rejection of a middle-class Negro simply on the basis of his color when all his other attributes, material and psychological, would qualify him for entrance into a life of middle-class security and social advantage. The stigma of blackness therefore assumes a special significance, distinct from the other stigmata of poverty, only at a time when the Negro is already moving out of poverty status. Until this point is reached, however, it is doubtful that the mark of blackness in itself exposes the Negro slum dweller to any more disadvantages than do his ragged and mismatched clothes or any other signs of poverty. Nor in the slum does his blackness handicap him any more than straight hair and high cheekbones handicap an Indian in a Dakota town.

Although each of the frequently mentioned attributes of the Negro poor we have thus far considered undoubtedly makes some small contribution to the pervasive but spurious notion that poverty is essentially a Negro problem, another highly important factor is often overlooked. This is the simple fact that whereas all other poor minorities are to a greater or less extent localized in one region or state in the country, Negroes live almost throughout the United States, in segregated but visible poverty. Eight or ten major cities from Texas to California recognize a Mexican problem (although there are many additional Mexicans in other cities around the country); a smaller number of generally smaller cities in the Southwest and northern Plains recognize an Indian problem; only Miami has a Cuban problem and only Honolulu a Samoan problem; but every city feels it has a Negro problem. As a consequence anyone who talks to or about Negroes immediately has a national audience. Correspondingly, everyone knows that many Negroes are poor because they have seen them with their own eyes, but relatively few people have any real conception of what proportion of Indians or Mexican-Americans or Hawaiians are rich or poor, to say nothing of knowing where they live or how, whether their families are typically stable or fatherless, or what kinds of jobs they are likely to hold, if any. A national consensus requires a national awareness. This is true whether the consensus is positive and contributes to the growth of our nation or whether it is, as here, negative and contributes only to a prejudiced stereotype.

The significance of the nation-wide distribution of Negroes becomes even more compelling when we recollect that the poverty program itself is, and indeed must be, a national program based essentially on federal initiative. In this context Negro poverty often becomes a convenient least common denominator in the many cause-and-effect equations which together define the multiple problems of poverty and their possible solutions. Also, although it is hard to assess its significance, the federally directed poverty programs are administered by people who reside and have their experiences of daily living in Washington, D.C., the only major city in the United States the majority of whose population is black.

Yet despite the attention given to those aspects of

the Negro dilemma which make black poverty a more conscious burden upon the national conscience than that of any other color, for our purposes they are less important than the fact that Negroes have generally adapted to the dictates of poverty in ways remarkably similar to those of other poor people. For civil rights leaders caught in their own personal as well as political no-man's-land between black and white it is understandable that emphasis should fall upon the distinctively Negro aspects of poverty. But if we are to understand the phenomenon of discrimination and its relationship to being poor so that we can use this understanding to refine our thinking about strategies, then our attention should be directed instead to the uniformities of poverty. These include not only a remarkable similarity in the way the life of poverty expresses itself among different minorities but also a quite uniform and consistently prejudicial response by the favored majority toward each of the poor minorities.

In the continuing interaction between haves and have-nots the discrepancy between them is not sustained merely through the denial to poor people of access to opportunities which the majority controls. Through legislation and through a variety of special programs this access can be provided. In many cases new avenues are already being opened up; as we have seen this is a central objective of the poverty program as it now stands. Beyond this, however, are the psychological dimensions of discrimination with which we are principally concerned in this chapter. In this domain lies the perception and evaluation of poor people and their lives by the wealthier majority. That this evaluation is negative is a fact widely known and widely deplored. It is, however, less common to find explicit recognition of the counterpart to this prejudice, namely the all too frequent acceptance by poor people themselves of the judgment of unworthiness which has been passed on them. As long as these negative assessments are shared by both participants in the unhappy interplay between the poor and the not-so-poor it is obvious that the mere removal of barriers to opportunity will not in itself assure upward mobility. It presumably was in part a recognition of this fact which led President Johnson to follow up the introduction of a mass of enabling civil rights legislation with a poverty program designed essentially to improve not only occupational skills but also the motivation and sense of self-worth necessary to move up into a world hopefully made permeable by the extension of equal rights to everyone.

Judgments of the poor are made by the richer majority on the basis of their seeing a life of poverty which is real and which is different. However, to this more or less accurate perception of an existing reality is then added the thoroughly unwarranted assumption that poor people live the way they do out of preference. This assumption is a key element in the structure of prejudice against the poor. Without it one would have to admit to the truth of the contention of social agencies and social scientists that the life style of poverty is something which is forced upon people by the very fact that they are poor. The fact that people are coerced into this life is attested by the uniformity in the response to poverty which we have seen which characterizes people of many diverse histories and cultures. But because the assumption of *willful* adherence by the poor to a deviant life style is crucial if the majority is to continue calling itself Christian while at the same time perpetuating a system of discrimination, the assumption will probably retain its vitality regardless of how much evidence is mobilized against it. It will probably disappear only when and if the life style itself disappears. Yet as we have seen most of the characteristics of this life style are themselves necessary and realistic adaptations to being poor. Thus we come once again to the nub of the problem of poverty: its evils cannot be corrected as long as people remain poor. The economics of poverty are thus a straitjacket which, like the straitjacket on a mental patient, not only restrains movement but also serves to stigmatize the wearer.

Yet the fact that being economically poor is central and probably antecedent to all other problems of poverty does not mean that we should plan strategies only in the economic realm. Once it comes into existence, prejudice takes its own toll and contributes to the perpetuation of any social problem regardless of its origin. Therefore, it is worthwhile briefly to review our conclusions for their relevance to strategies of intervention against prejudice as such.

Discrimination is at root a psychological phenomenon upon which is then erected an assortment of social mechanisms designed to enforce its value judgments. It is triggered by symbolically significant behaviors on the part of the victims of prejudice, including such things as habits of speech, of dress, hygiene and posture. One strategy for reducing the frequency with which enforcing mechanisms are called into play then consists in identifying these triggering behaviors and altering them or reducing their frequency. Several existing poverty programs already include these behaviors among their explicit targets, teaching people (as in the Job Corps) how to present themselves to the world in a middle-class way.

Unfortunately, however, as we have just noted, the subjective value judgments of prejudice achieve their discriminatory effects not only through actions taken by the dominant majority, but all too often also because the targets of prejudice themselves accept the judgment of their own unworthiness. This is especially likely among poor people whose very poverty is itself a sign of failure. Inevitably this leads to a sense of personal worthlessness and lack of motivation to strive, or even such certainty of continuing failure that the whole idea of trying for a change in status is frightening. Less anguished but equally crippling are the psychological orientations which result from a sense of being powerless and hopeless, at once trapped and sheltered in a small familiar corner of the world: a limited future time orientation, inability to delay gratification or to plan ahead, a concrete view of the immediate environment with almost no appreciation of the larger world, and an unreadiness really to trust anyone. These dimensions of discrimination which reside principally in the psychology of its ghettoed victims are the ones toward which the present poverty programs have particularly directed their energies. Consequently they embrace far more than just job training. A great deal of compassion and psychological sophistication have gone into the design of program elements intended to improve assurance and a sense of personal worth, to teach the more subtle interpersonal skills expected by middle-class employers and neighbors, to explicate a larger world view, to instill a sense of pride in one's self and what one stands for, and to create a sense of team endeavor in struggling to rise above the constraints of poverty. These programs will be discussed at greater length in the next chapter. Many of them are brilliantly conceived and if they have fallen short of their goals it is probably due less to their inherent design than it is to the limitation of the opportunities which have been opened up for graduates from the programs.

The other half of the picture is seen in the psychological mechanisms which operate within the discriminating majority of the population. Some of these are completely irrational and based upon stereotypes unrelated to reality. An example of this is the arrogant assumption on the part of many white people that all Negro men want to marry their daughters. Other perceptions do have some basis in reality. Thus it is true that an uneducated poor person with poor impulse control and lacking in self-confidence is unlikely to be able to assume a responsible occupational role. Prejudice enters in, however, when the further assumption is made that everyone who is poor or even looks poor shares these qualities and probably cannot change them. Here some success has been experienced through programs and policies which insist that everyone be given a fair try at fulfilling whatever positions may be open and only be rejected as the result of demonstrated failure.

These programs have been launched principally under the banner of civil rights and as such have been directed principally toward the enfranchisement of Negroes, although the legal language potentially embraces all kinds of people. A major difficulty with this strategy has been that it entails a substantial amount of risk. As we have just seen, effective adaptation of poor people to the life of poverty is usually achieved only at the price of acquiring behaviors which simultaneously curtail their ability to function adaptively in the more affluent context of a steady job. Therefore, no matter how we might wish it otherwise, opening up employment to all comers does in fact increase the failure rate — and it takes only a few failures to reinforce all of the stereotypes upon which prejudice rests, whereas new and more positive stereotypes seem to be built only upon an overwhelming number of successes. The inevitable consequence of this imbalance is that even conscientious program administrators in order to show a reasonable level of success are forced to engage in the game of "skimming," taking only the best bets off the top, those who already are closest to middle-class norms in their behavior, appearance and outlook. The really poor and the really hopeless are thus once again left behind, still without money and still without hope.

It is questionable whether equal rights and equal

opportunities can ever be achieved entirely through regulatory and programmatic legislation. Problems of skimming and of backlash have already demonstrated the extreme difficulty of the task. The weakness in any program of enforcement rests in the fact that any system short of total dictatorship cannot cope with a situation in which a large number of people are unsympathetic with the goals of enforcement. A classic case in our recent history was Prohibition. Assuredly civil rights programs command a far greater consensus than did the Eighteenth Amendment but it seems likely that in the foreseeable future neither civil rights nor the War on Poverty will develop a sufficient consensus to become effectively self-enforcing.

The only way in which this can happen is that the stereotype of the poor, collectively and in all the various poor minorities, be radically and positively redefined. In the last chapter we saw the dramatic results of a positive definition when we considered the status of veterans under the GI Bill. The veterans of course did not start out with a negative stereotype, yet if the GI Bill had not defined their rights in such positive fashion it is probable that they would have been forgotten as rapidly and completely as were the veterans of World War I who fifteen years later became the Bonus Marchers camping on the mud flats of Anacostia. More radical changes in ethnic stereotype from negative to positive are, however, also possible. Such changes actually befell both Japanese and Chinese people on the West Coast during the years in which we were alternately friends and enemies with their countries of origin. In fact the Chinese, who had been imported in large numbers to build railroads and to provide labor during the Gold Rush in California, but subsequently became a competitive threat in the labor market, were initially described in terms very reminiscent of those which are now used to dehumanize our poverty-stricken minorities. Later, of course, when the Japanese overran China and the Chinese were seen as heroically defending themselves against our common enemy, their fellows on the West Coast were abruptly exalted in status, and given an image of industry, honesty, and frugality to match.

A similar discrepancy in definition often differentiates attitudes toward American-born Negroes from those applied to representatives of African countries. Even though the American Negro is more likely to speak English well and to know better the manners of the land, even the most rigid segregationists from the South were almost from the beginning prepared to accept people from African nations, once they were so identified, for service in restaurants or on any of the other early testing grounds of integration. Indeed for a while it appeared that the symbolic alternative which African identity offered might in some way be capitalized upon to redefine the role of American Negroes. This possibility was examined with guarded optimism a few years ago by Harold Isaacs, but subsequent events showed it to be an empty hope.*

Neither politicians nor social scientists have yet found the means to change negative stereotypes to positive, to convert contempt into respect. Nor, despite our protestations of love for our neighbor, does it appear likely that we will extend a truly helping hand to persons we have defined as unworthy. Thus it seems that prejudice and discrimination will continue to present serious roadblocks both to the effectiveness of programs against poverty and to the legislative enactment of these programs. The progress that is made will be hewn always out of resistant rock. Far too much of the labor and sacrifice which this will cost will inevitably be expended by those who are themselves victims of the system which we are trying to change, although for their misfortunes we, not they, stand responsible. Nevertheless, if it is possible consistently to bear in mind that the problems not only of poverty but also of prejudice are shared with remarkable uniformity by almost all poor people regardless of their history or culture, we

* Harold R. Isaacs, *The New World of Negro Americans* (New York: John Day, 1963).

can better see the commonality of their problems. Out of this we may be able to apply the experience of one to the benefit of another. From this cumulation of wisdom we may in time begin to discern the shape of the strategies which will be necessary to make more real the brotherhood of man, not only between black and white but also between rich and poor.

6

Poverty Is Being Incompetent

Among the strategic implications of the idea of a *culture* of poverty one stands out most clearly: if poverty is both the cause and result of a way of life in which self-defeating behaviors are learned by each rising generation, then any attack on poverty should try to modify these behaviors. Put more positively this cultural conception of poverty means that if its cycle is to be broken poor people must among other things be taught new and more effective ways of functioning. We have already noted that the concept of the culture of poverty forms a key element in the intellectual underpinnings of the War on Poverty. It is therefore not surprising that skill training occupies an important if not central place in the poverty programs.

Not only do a substantial proportion of poverty funds go into programs designed to increase social and occupational competence, but these programs take a wide diversity of forms, underscoring the large amount of creative thought which has been devoted to this aspect of the overall task of combating poverty. Broadly speaking, they fall into three general types. First there are a series of programs concerned with occupational training. Although all of these undertake to teach specific job skills, most of them go well beyond this limited objective in an effort to create more appropriate motivation, self-awareness, and self-confidence, and to train for the complex and often intangible interpersonal skills which are so essential to obtaining and holding a good job. Many of these programs are highly sophisticated and range from formal training facilities such as Job Corps Centers to a variety of apprentice and similar on-the-job training programs. All of these take very seriously the admonition of psychologists and social scientists who have studied poor people that successful employment means a great deal more than just technical skill in a given job. Thus the poverty programs concerned with training of manpower, although administered by a number of different agencies, have in common a concern with developing fully productive members of the labor force who display not only the necessary technical competence but also equally essential elements of social competence.

The second type of program aimed at social competence emphasizes the achievement of formal educational goals. Some are directed almost entirely toward academic achievement. Best known among these is Project Head Start at the preschool level, but there are a number of others, operating mostly within school systems, which are intended both to enhance existing performance at all levels and also to recapture and rehabilitate academic failures. The latter include the well-known high school dropout programs, and a number of programs in the area of adult education. Often educational activities for adolescents and adults are combined with the occupational and social training programs described above, as for example in the Job Corps, in work-study programs, in the Department of Defense draft rejectee program, and many others. Again, these educationally oriented activities have drawn heavily upon the behavioral sciences and have pioneered and utilized a variety of highly sophisticated educational procedures. Project Head Start, for example, although now the subject of some critical second thoughts, at its launching was almost universally acclaimed as a major effort to apply the knowledge derived from research on the effects of early environmental enrichment.[*]

[*] See, J. McVicker Hunt, "The Psychological Basis for Using Pre-School Enrichment as an Antidote for Cultural Deprivation," *The*

A third rather specialized type of program trains and utilizes people who are themselves poor to work in subprofessional roles with other poor people in urban ghettos. These so-called indigenous workers are expected to make a contribution to achievement of the objectives of the agencies which hire them, but they are expected also to be able to capitalize upon their experience for their own self-improvement. The strategy of using indigenous workers therefore deserves a place in the roster of programs intended to enhance social competence, but in both philosophy and administration it is quite separate from the other training and educational programs and will be treated separately later in this chapter. The indigenous worker activities taken together add up to a rather smaller operation than the major investment in money and manpower represented by the other social competence program areas.

By now a substantial amount of experience has been accumulated with these programs. Some preliminary evaluations have been attempted, and the verdicts have in general not been encouraging. In addition there have been a few well publicized expressions of protest, particularly involving Job Corps centers. It is probably significant that these have

Merrill-Palmer Quarterly, 10 (1964), 209–248. This paper was written well before the inception of Head Start, but summarizes most of the evidence upon which the program was based.

generally not received treatment in the press nearly as sympathetic as that which is often accorded to demonstrations and even riots in urban areas. In a blunt but fairly typical critique, Cloward and Ontell looked at youth employment programs from the vantage point of the Mobilization for Youth, a richly staffed pioneering poverty project with a large research and evaluation component. They were so discouraged by the prospects that they concluded social agencies were doing nothing more in youth employment training than "helping the society to engineer a massive illusion."[*]

Is it really that bad? The fact that poor people are socially, occupationally and academically relatively lacking in competence and therefore unable to get good jobs is certainly in itself no illusion. Are we then kidding ourselves that we know how to train people in order to improve their skills? The programs which have been undertaken have consistently availed themselves to the fullest of the understandings we have of the causes of the social and intellectual deficits of the poor, and the techniques being employed have in many cases been the subject of considerable experimentation and empirical validation. It is hard to believe that all this presumably scientifically based knowledge is illusory. Cloward

[*] Richard A. Cloward and Robert Ontell, "Our Illusions About Training," *American Child*, 47, No. 1 (January, 1965), 6–10.

and Ontell themselves in the end suggest that the principal ingredient in the illusion is the realistic lack of jobs in sufficient numbers and at sufficiently high levels to make possible the work careers for which the young people in these programs are purportedly being readied. It is specifically because they do not see a prospect for an increase in these jobs that they end on a note of discouragement, but they appear prepared to generalize from this to reject the entire strategy. One quality which seldom characterizes criticism of the War on Poverty is temperance.

It is undoubtedly true that the employment programs have not been as successful in placing people in permanent jobs as their early protagonists hoped and promised. Yet it also seems premature to write them off. In fact we cannot. We cannot sit back, saying we have tried our best, and wait for the coming of the utopian day when there will once again be a plenitude of those unskilled manufacturing jobs which our forefathers used as stepping-stones to full participation in the good life of the American melting pot. The problem of poverty in the 1960's has assumed its present dimensions precisely because the market for unskilled labor can no longer provide either the jobs or the security necessary to absorb the socially disadvantaged and untrained people who are now migrating to the cities — no longer from Europe but from our own depressed areas in the United States. What our experience to date with poverty programs has clearly demonstrated is that we will never meet the social problems created by the new technologies as long as we think of preparation for employment and employment itself in essentially traditional terms. At least two major changes seem to be indicated, one in the programs themselves and the other in the larger society. First let us look at the change within training programs.

Preparation for employment is the central objective in most of these programs. As we have noted they are remarkably sophisticated in their concern with the broad range of skills and knowledge necessary to obtain and hold a job. People are trained how to talk, how to look, how to behave, and how to inform themselves about job prospects. One would be hard pressed to identify an area of necessary knowledge which has been left out of the training programs designed to help unemployed and unemployable poor people. However, the other half of the picture, the formidable emotional hurdles which have to be surmounted in order to first become employable and then steadily employed, are largely overlooked. Most of us can probably still remember the first time we ever applied for a job — not only the uncertainty of it all but the anguish lest we be tried and found wanting, particularly by some interviewer who did not in himself seem of great enough stature to justify his possessing the power to decide our destiny. If the experience can be so traumatic even for those of us in the well-educated middle class, how much worse it must be for a person reared in a climate of discouragement and despair and only recently and uncertainly equipped with the minimally necessary social skills. Furthermore, this person receives his hearing before an interviewer who seems truly powerful because he comes of different and more privileged antecedents.

A prior and equally critical trial is in store for a young person who enters the Job Corps. He leaves his home neighborhood, a place which may not be joyous but whose threats and dangers are at least familiar, and enters a large institutional complex full of people of obvious authority and uncertain demands. He also finds himself among other people, contemporaries in age and background, who in another setting would have to be met and challenged before mutual acceptance would be possible.

Farther down the road when training is completed and a poor person finally enters into a hopefully steady job, after the first few days have passed and people have stopped making allowances for his inexperience, he rapidly discovers he must meet an array of new obligations and expectations, withstand new temptations, and cope effectively with new challenges not only to his competence but also to his self-respect.

Without multiplying these examples further it is evident that for a poor person getting and holding a job takes a lot more than the combination of technical and social skills which together constitute the bulk of present employment assistance programs. The essential program ingredient which is missing is emotional support through all the difficult steps toward employment. To achieve the goal of his training, a person must drive himself through a change in status so complete that after years of seeing himself as worthless, incompetent, and unwanted he can persuade himself and the world that he is a productive, competent, and valued member of an enterprise and of his community. Some of the programs have made a partial attempt to provide the needed psychological support by offering a set of experiences in which challenges increase only gradually in their severity and success is simultaneously experienced with sufficient frequency to create a growing sense of accomplishment and self-worth. However, even this is not enough. There is much more to the radical changes in role which the poverty training programs demand than merely occupational adjustment and occupational satisfaction. There is for example loneliness, the threat of the unknown, and a demand for initiative when before one learned that safety lay only in obscurity. Taken together these result in a great reluctance to stand up and make one's way in a world which heretofore has been consistently hostile and in which one has invariably lost every round.

The kind of support needed to persevere through the ordeal of trying to change from a loser to a winner can probably be most fully supplied by the techniques of mental health. Although the traditional responsibility of mental health has been to treat psychological casualties once they have been diagnosed as damaged, an increasing amount of attention is now being devoted to more positive supportive activities, usually as adjuncts to programs with different primary objectives. Quite recently attention has been directed specifically toward mental health intervention of this kind with the poor.* Over the years, however, other kinds of psychiatric programs have been developed to meet needs in many ways similar to those of a poor person who for the first time tries to conquer his incapacity and stand up to face the world. Thus for example amputees, the blind, and other handicapped persons not only receive physical devices which make possible more normal functions. They also receive counselling and other therapies, both individual and

* Quentin A. F. Rae-Grant, Thomas Gladwin, and Eli M. Bower, "Mental Health, Social Competence and the War on Poverty," *American Journal of Orthopsychiatry*, 36 (1966), 652–664.

group, designed to help them understand and surmount their anxieties and adapt effectively to a new self and way of life. Another example even closer to the model of the poor person entering the world of work is the patient (often poor) who leaves a mental hospital and goes out into the world. He struggles under the double burden of his stigma and of the knowledge that he has at least once before broken under the strain. Considerable experience has been accumulated with programs to prepare patients emotionally for this experience and to follow and support them as they are going through it. Although not entirely lacking, comparable support is seldom available to poor people who leave the asylum of poverty after not just one or two experiences of failure but rather a whole lifetime of it.

However, mental health techniques cannot make the real world seem different than it is. As a result there is very little which psychiatry or any other profession can do to relieve the emotional damage of despair as long as no real solutions exist for the problems which create the despair. Thus mental health can do very little for the problems of poverty except in conjunction with other programs which remove the barriers to opportunity, the root cause of most of the emotional problems of the poor. But even within this limitation mental health people and mental health know-how have not made the contribution they could have. Mental health techniques are not magic, but it is safe to say that enough knowledge presently exists with which to assure a marked increase in the ratio of training successes over failures. Furthermore, programs such as those for returning mental hospital patients have demonstrated that the required supportive procedures can be implemented by people with relatively limited mental health training, provided they are specifically oriented toward this particular task. This, then, is one respect at least in which we have not yet done all we know how to do in order to prepare people and sustain them through the rigors of entering for the first time the ranks of the employed.

There remains, however, the other side of the coin, the problem which Cloward and Ontell confronted without finding any solution. This is the fact that enough jobs realistically no longer exist to provide adequate employment for people who must begin their careers at a relatively low level of skill and of responsibility. The jobs which do exist are furthermore of a sort more than usually likely to be psychologically damaging. For example, in many cities the majority of the regular unskilled jobs which are open can be filled only by women, thus upsetting the culturally favored family structure in which the man is expected to be the breadwinner. This dilemma has frequently been documented for

Puerto Rican families in New York where only women can find employment in the garment trades. It is also seen in other ethnic groups (e.g., Mexicans and Negroes) for whom the most commonly available jobs are in domestic service and thus open again only to women. Many other kinds of unskilled employment, although open to men, are seen as menial if not actually degrading and thus tend to neutralize such little self-respect as the mere fact of employment can contribute. This is true of trash collectors and cleaning crews and others whose work involves dealing with the refuse of others, and equally true of common laborers on construction projects who forever hold a shovel and are never allowed to touch a hammer.

What are we to do about these people? One statistical projection after another assures us the time will never come again when there will be jobs for all and jobs which all can handle. If this is true then it is clearly unrealistic, as Cloward and Ontell insist, to continue to prepare people for low level jobs when they know, and we know, there will never be enough of this kind of work to go around. Therefore if we are to do anything other than to throw up our hands in despair we must look anew at the problem, and this time we had better be sure we look at the real and central problem. This is: How can more jobs, and more psychologically constructive jobs with permanency and a future, be created in a world in which all of the productive industries are becoming more and more automated, and it therefore seems that the number of jobs for which the poor can realistically be expected to be prepared are steadily becoming fewer? Put differently, what we should be looking at is the structure of the labor market itself. We should be inquiring whether there are ways it might be changed so that its demand for labor will more closely match the available supply. Until we do this we stand guilty once again of fighting the new war with the weapons and strategies of the old.

In the rationalized systems of technology and production for which the United States is justly famous, needs for skilled manpower rarely go unmet at any level. There are always qualified young men ready to step up to vice-president, co-pilots ready to become pilots, and men ready to man the production lines of Detroit in whatever numbers are necessary to turn out the predetermined quota of cars for each month. Rapid changes in technology or unexpected demands in the marketplace (as in time of war) may create occasional shortages in certain categories of labor, but in an impressively rapid and efficient set of phased responses the unions open up positions for a few more apprentices, increases in overtime pay lead to adjustments in pay scales, and technological innovations are made when necessary, as for example to compensate for lack of tool-and-diemakers whose training takes too long.

When we turn, however, to the service trades, and equally to the service professions, we find exactly the opposite obtains. Even those professions which are high in pay and status, of which medicine is an outstanding example, suffer from chronic shortages and inefficient delivery. Regardless of their ability to pay, people in a number of circumstances cannot obtain medical services witout great delay and inconvenience. There is an acute and growing shortage of qualified doctors both in rural areas and on the staffs of large hospitals. Similarly, the gravely ill can often not obtain bedside nursing. In another particularly senseless contradiction, we talk constantly about the growing importance of education and yet continue to do practically nothing about raising the pay and status of teachers. Dropping below the professional level, who has not taken his car into a garage for service in the morning and stood around in the company of a number of highly paid and responsible people waiting with enforced patience for the service manager to pay them some heed? Finally, what suburban family would not pay twice as much if they could be sure of having the house cleaned when it needed to be cleaned, baby-sitters when they are needed, and the lawn mowed whenever it reached a certain height? Examples could be multiplied from anyone's everyday experience to demonstrate that, with a few exceptions such as salesmen, barbers, and sometimes secretaries, services which are delivered in person are likely to be provided unreliably, often impolitely, seemingly more at the convenience of the server than the served, and yet paradoxically by people who, aside from the higher level professions, are generally underpaid and given little reward in status for the magnitude of their responsibility or the value of their contribution to society.

What this all means is that the service occupations comprise a vast sector of our labor force which is irrationally utilized and often inadequately trained and ineffectively recruited. Although with our ever growing affluence more and more people have been able to afford the services which provide employment for this unrationalized sector of our labor economy, they have thus far apparently been willing to suffer its inefficiencies without organized revolt. They put up with inconvenience and often indignity to obtain needed services and often pay extravagantly for them besides. They seem to comfort themselves only with rather lame jokes and shared anecdotes about TV repairmen, cleaning women and "society" doctors.

But bad jokes will not forever paper over the glaring contrast between, on the one hand, a steady reduction in the need for those classes of labor which are recruited through rational and efficient technological channels, and, on the other, the equally steady but poorly met growth in demands for services by people who can afford to pay for them. This contrast is of course relevant to the problems of poverty and chronic unemployment because solutions to the current inefficiency in the provision of services would carry with them massive opportunities for employment of people without requiring extensive prior technical and professional training. The form which such solutions should take is, however, far from self-evident. To bring the often low status, low paid and always haphazardly organized service occupations up to the level of the systematically manned technical and productive sectors will comprise a major achievement in social engineering.

Thus far, although the inevitability of a shift in the bulk of the labor force from production to service employment is widely recognized, very little progress has been made in laying out the avenues along which this movement can be expected to flow. Scattered efforts to organize the delivery of services in a way which will more nearly meet the needs of the consumer have thus far proven largely unavailing. Correspondingly, discovery of means whereby service occupations could be made to provide worthwhile and satisfactory career opportunities have also proven illusive. Perhaps the difficulty lies in a failure to recognize that this is essentially a new problem with new dimensions, and therefore one for which new solutions must be sought. At least it is clear by now that the old mechanisms for adjusting labor resources to meet new needs are not working effectively in the service area and new strategies must therefore be found. Since the problem is essentially one of workers no longer responding to new needs for labor, at least in ways which are satisfactory either to them or to the consumers of their output, the first place to look is the relationship of the worker to his work and the meaning of work in the service as against the production occupations.

The production worker, around whom our traditional concepts of labor utilization have been built, deals primarily with things rather than with people. "Things" includes not only tools and other tangible objects in the blue collar domain, but also the paperwork through which white collar workers make their contribution. The different kinds of production work have in common only that judgments are in the last analysis not concerned primarily with human welfare but with rather mechanical efficiency, profit and other concrete material standards. Not surprisingly, in service of these goals, the organization of labor initially took the form of craft unions primarily for blue collar workers. The members of each craft served a restricted range of specialized functions.

Regardless of the considerable benefits which their members may have derived from affiliation with them, these craft unions contributed to the overall production process principally as a means for supplying sufficient numbers of trained and qualified workers in each occupational category. To some extent this tradition still obtains, as for example in the building trades where there are apprentice programs to develop labor resources, and unions rather than employers have a principal voice in determining the qualifications of workers for specific tasks. Management defined their needs for labor in terms of occupational categories corresponding to union jurisdictions. Nominally at least one human being was considered the equivalent of another provided he had similar formal qualifications in his work specialty. Labor economists, government statisticians and other analysts of the labor market accepted from labor and management these occupational categories as the principal dimensions to be used in analyzing the recruitment and deployment of labor resources. This practice of analyzing work on the basis of occupational skills continues to the present day, even though the structure of labor unions has long since been radically altered away from its original occupational basis.

This alteration came about through the introduction of industrial unions. The industrial union, among other things, no longer plays a major role in recruitment and training of workers. Stripped of these responsibilities, it is left with a major concern *only* for pay, conditions of employment, security, and other factors which have in common a primary concern with the welfare of the worker as a human being. In this context it is incidentally not surprising that it has been the large industrial unions which have done the most in projecting labor into the human issues such as poverty and civil rights. In contrast the skill-oriented building trades have proved most reactionary on these issues. Industrial unions also include increasing numbers of service workers employed in large enterprises to meet the needs of the community of employees which exist there. They have thus already begun to address themselves, often in bewilderment, to the new kinds of work relationships which these service occupations imply.

There has of course been a corresponding change on upper levels. Whereas in the past management could use profit as a straightforward and relatively uncomplicated basis for judgment, and supervisors could equally respond primarily to canons of productive efficiency, now they have learned to think also in more human and psychological terms of image and morale, and the loyalty of customers and employees.

Already one wonders whether an analysis of the

deployment of labor in terms principally of occupational specialties is adequate to meet even these issues of concern to management. If we look beyond this to its adequacy for analysis of the dilemmas arising from the growth of the service occupations, it is immediately obvious that its utility is extremely limited. This has been demonstrated pragmatically by the general failure on the part of labor economists and other professionals to devise effective ways for relieving the many difficulties experienced by both the service worker and his client. More substantively, if one looks at the kind of work which is implied in most service occupations it is clear that the occupational specialty is much less important in determining the satisfaction felt by both the producer and consumer of services than are the more personal and interpersonal factors which surround the work situation and determine the way in which the service is delivered and received. These include not only formal conditions of employment but also factors of status, dominance and submission, dignity, respect, independence and the like. Service occupations almost by definition are centered upon relationships between people, one person doing something with or for another.

This necessarily means that a psychological dimension is introduced into the work process. There have of course always been psychological aspects to any employment, as Charlie Chaplin effectively demonstrated many years ago in *Modern Times*. However, in the industrial sector this was seen as sufficiently minor that it could be ignored without interfering with productivity. An essential difference between production work and service work is that the psychological dimension in the latter is sufficiently influential that it cannot be ignored. It may indeed be primary in determining whether any particular kind of service will be adequately rendered. Put in a different way, the efficiency with which goods are produced can be judged without primary reference either to the producer or the consumer as human beings, whereas the adequacy with which a service is rendered must necessarily involve psychological judgments about the perceptions, feelings, and responses of both server and served. From the standpoint of the consumer, a rude waiter can spoil an otherwise excellent meal and a hostile doctor can do a patient more harm than good simply by getting him upset. Equally, the service worker may be well paid and well trained but dislike his job because it is lacking in dignity or respectability. The personal satisfaction of both thus becomes a major element in judging the efficiency of any kind of person-to-person service work.

Therefore, the first step toward developing programs which will provide satisfactory service and satisfying service employment is to gain an understanding of the psychological implications of different kinds of service relationships. Of course simply stating this does not bring us to any immediate resolution of the problems we are facing, but then neither in the past did a recognition that occupational categories are key elements in allocating productive labor in itself rationalize industrial employment. It did, however, define the avenues of inquiry which had to be pursued in order to assure that labor resources would be more effectively exploited. In similar fashion, then, we must look at the psychological dimensions of service employment if we hope to rationalize this area of activity. Only in this way can we develop the knowledge necessary to meet the need for more services in our affluent society and more jobs for those people who still suffer in a world of poverty.

There are many things we need to know. We need to understand why some service jobs are seen as respectable and even attractive while others with similar characteristics are responded to in quite opposite fashion. Why, for example, is selling generally considered to be a good occupation to enter even though it is rare to find a rich salesman, and a salesman must always be submissive and subservient, humbling himself before everyone who comes in the door as an "always right" customer? Conversely, why do other people go into occupations which are generally considered somewhat less than respectable? Barbering is, for example, an occupation which is not generally looked upon as very distinguished and yet a lot of people go into it. Why is this? Is it perhaps because barbering offers unusual opportunities for establishing one's own small business after a few years of hard work? If so, should barbering be classed for some purposes along with being a plumber, where similar opportunities often present themselves for establishing a business after a few years? The barber and the plumber are very different in their occupational specialties but it may be useful to think of them as having many career interests in common and therefore similar motivations regarding their employment.

Barbering invites other interesting speculations. Training to become a barber is frequently obtained at a "barber college." Barber colleges are strictly occupational training schools similar to those established for many other trades, but giving them the prestigious name of "college" may have a significant impact on persons trying to make up their minds regarding future careers. Also barbers have been able to maintain a higher level of compensation for their services than many other similar occupations largely through rather effective organizations. Usually these are organized as unions and given this name, but they are in fact commonly a kind of trade association different in many respects from a traditional union. Does this suggest a prototype for new and different kinds of organizations of labor more appropriate to the service area? It may be significant that thus far relatively few traditionally organized labor unions have developed to any substantial degree among service workers, although the Retail Clerks International Association is a notable exception.

We need also to understand much more than we presently do about the way services are viewed by consumers. Sometimes the behavior of people who clearly want and need a variety of services appears to be almost deliberately self-defeating. Why do people who complain about the lack of traffic enforcement and dangerous drivers on the highways themselves so often employ deception, harassment and insulting epithets in their own relationships with traffic police, thus actively discouraging qualified people from making this their career? Why do householders who characteristically complain about the problem of getting their lawns mowed seem determined only to recruit as mowers neighborhood kids who will accept less than a minimum wage, even though as a consequence they then have to spend a lot of other money buying a power mower and stay home on Saturdays to mow the lawn themselves? Why when education has been exalted to a primary place among our national institutions is there such strong continuing resistance to paying teachers salaries commensurate with their training, skills, and responsibilities? From these few examples it should be obvious that whereas market research has taught us a great deal about how to design commercial products in order to please consumers we know practically nothing about the principles which govern consumer behavior in the service areas. Since any service operation is an interpersonal transaction, the most critical determinants of its adequacy and efficiency are the premises with which both server and served enter into the transaction.

Although the potentially full utilization of the growing millions of unemployed and underemployed in the United States must await genuine rationalization of service occupations in the private sector, challenging opportunities for experimentation lie immediately before us in public programs. These arise from the rapidly expanding needs for personal services in a variety of largely government-sponsored health and welfare programs. Medicare, Medicaid, programs for children, the aged, the mentally ill and retarded, recreation activities, and many others currently being planned will require vast amounts of manpower in essentially service roles. Estimates run up to three to five million new jobs to be created.

137

The success of these new programs will depend heavily on the degree of flexibility and creativity which goes into the development of this pool of manpower. If for example arbitrary and exclusive eligibility rules are broadened, by civil service, by unions, and by professional organizations then new reservoirs of competent personnel will at once become available for career training and recruitment. If in addition the service positions are analyzed and filled on the basis of their psychological as well as their technical qualities we could move with these initial programs in the public sector a long way toward better methods of utilization of service workers generally.

Many questions need to be answered and wholly new strategies must be designed, tested and proven before the enormous employment potential of the service occupations can be fully realized. As long as the majority of service jobs pay less than their production equivalents and many of them are seen as second class employment suitable only for second-rate workers, and as long as neither security nor career potential exists in most of them and there are no effective organizations to serve and protect the interest of the servers, just so long as these conditions persist we in the affluent sector will continue to wait to obtain the services we want and are presumably able to pay for, and at the same time multitudes of potentially available poor people will remain unemployed because the avenues for recruitment into the needed jobs are either nonexistent or actively distasteful to them.

Turning now to education, the second major area of competence which poverty programs strive to augment, much less needs to be said with respect to either the philosophy or the basic strategies around which programs have been designed. It has long been recognized that an intimate cause-and-effect relationship operates in both directions between poverty and lack of education. At every level, the children of poor families are lower in both educational performance and participation. At the same time it is equally evident that education is probably the single most critical factor in determining eligibility for employment of almost any kind. Accordingly programs have been developed reaching all the way from preschool preparation under Project Head Start through work-study support for students in college and literacy classes for adults. A number of these operate in various ways to combine formal education with work training and experience. These combination programs seem to be effective in motivating and retaining students who are able to handle neither school nor a job alone on a full-time basis. Thus they fill a real need for people not yet ready for a regular academic program.

Planning of educational programs for the poor has sometimes been criticized as too limited in scope. It is proposed that one thing or another be appended to the basic educational objectives in order to obtain a larger return on the investment. Undoubtedly some of the elements experimentally added to a few programs have contributed extra benefits without compromising the basic educational objectives. For example the parental participation requirement of Head Start, especially in rural areas, has often helped to organize and lend authority to people previously almost entirely mute in their distress. However, in general it can be said that the importance of educational enhancement is so great that it must not be compromised. Since it carries with it sufficient problems of its own the wisdom of adding to its complexities deserves seriously to be questioned.

Criticisms are also leveled at the efficacy and appropriateness of one particular program or technique in comparison with another. However, with a few exceptions, of which Head Start is again an example, most of the educational programs supported under the War on Poverty envision a relatively immediate payoff. It is therefore relatively easy to discern effective and ineffective strategies and to make corrections accordingly. Most of these educational programs consequently have a built-in self-correcting quality, or at least should have if their proponents are honest in evaluating their achievements.

At only one point should words of caution perhaps be expressed. This is with respect to programmed instruction and other often imaginative gadgetry designed to supplement or occasionally to bypass normal classroom procedures in order to convey as much curriculum content as possible in the least amount of time and with the smallest investment of scarce trained professional manpower. Many of these techniques are demonstrably successful in attaining their stated goals. Prodigious amounts of learning are sometimes achieved by people with formerly poor academic records. Caution is necessary not because this new technology is ineffective, but rather because of the limited scope of its effectiveness. These methods principally teach content, plus some of the more straightforward logical skills required to manipulate this content. When viewed broadly, however, education consists in much more than learning specific content and academic skills. The three R's are of course important, as anyone who does not know them can readily testify. But viewed from the standpoint, for example, of a prospective employer, much of the content of formal curriculum especially at the high school level makes essentially no contribution to job performance. Few employers will expect that people they hire on the basis of their high school diplomas will actually be solving algebraic equations on the job, or dwelling upon the fine points of American history with customers who come in off the street.

But there is more to schooling than this. Earning a high school diploma requires at least a minimum of intelligence and persistence and some willingness to conform, plus such congenial secondary qualities as politeness and neatness. It is principally these characteristics which the employer reads into an employee's high school diploma, not a familiarity with Shakespeare or the Pythogorean theorem. Our educational system is a complex socializing institution. When its stamp of approval is placed upon a student as he graduates from one stage to another the school is certifying not just to the content which examination grades show he has learned, but also to the attainment of a rather broad set of maturational goals. The fact that these goals may be arrived at more through dogged persistence on the part of a student than as a result of deliberate character-building efforts by the teachers is beside the point. The real point is that neither character-building nor dogged persistence are necessarily involved in learning by means of the newer and more sophisticated psychological techniques. Thus although they may be invaluable in making up specific academic deficits, they are not a substitute for years of sociali-

zation in school, including the give-and-take of classroom experience with its inevitable frustrations, with
its acceptance of occasional humiliation, and hopefully with some sense of personal intellectual challenge. Programmed instruction has real value in
correcting many of the intellectual deficits which
arise from a life of poverty. Its true worth can,
however, best be realized if we recognize its definite
limitations and understand that it is not the panacea
some believe it to be.

The third and last major strategy concerned with
developing social competence and a sense of self-
worth among poor people involves the utilization of
poor people themselves to supplement the work of
professional staffs in a variety of community
agencies. These people are usually referred to as
indigenous workers or indigenous nonprofessionals.*
It might be mentioned in passing that the word
"indigenous" is felt by some to have a condescending
quality. This would, however, be more objectionable
if poor people better understood its implications.
The effect might then be comparable to what one
might expect if the principal of a suburban school
were to refer to the members of the PTA as his

* Robert Reiff and Frank Riessman, *The Indigenous Nonprofessional: A Strategy of Change in a Community Action and Community Mental Health Programs,* National Institute of Labor Education, Mental Health Program Report No. 3 (New York, 1964).

"indigenous nonprofessionals." Be that as it may this strategy has been widely used in a variety of community programs for poor people. Part of its attraction unquestionably derives from its intent both to enhance the effectiveness of programs in which the workers are employed and at the same time to give to them a sense of worth and dignity deriving from their association with professionals in the cause of helping their less fortunate confreres. Although at first glance this dual argument in support of the indigenous worker strategy is very persuasive, both of its elements are open to serious question.

The principal rationale for supplementing the staff of social agencies by recruitment of subprofessional aides, in addition to the obvious advantage of relieving shortages of trained manpower, is the presumption that poor people can communicate better with other poor people than can self-conscious middle-class professionals. There is undoubtedly some truth in this view. However, experience suggests that as the indigenous worker becomes more identified with agency programs and objectives and is thus enabled to shoulder an increasing load of responsibility, he simultaneously becomes increasingly alienated from the poor people with whom he was originally identified. In an effort to counter this trend some agencies have adopted the policy of insisting that their indigenous workers remain in residence in the area, usually an urban slum, from which they were re-cruited and in which they will continue to work. However, since most people trapped in urban ghettos see their own salvation to lie in an escape from this same environment, they are chagrined to discover that when for the first time in their lives they have the resources to move elsewhere, the hand which gives them these resources simultaneously takes away the right to use them in the only way which they see as meaningful.

Often a more subtle psychological process is also at work, in which the person fortunate enough to move upward looks back with scorn at the misery recently left behind. It is the same process which, as we noted in the last chapter, helps dilute the leadership of minority ethnic groups. Although it is by no means characteristic of all, or even a majority, of indigenous workers, when it occurs it can be most invidious. Here it takes the form of over-identifying with one kind of social work role, the stance of a wise and admonishing, but condescending, parent. This is a stance which most professional workers try mightily to avoid, but even they are not always completely successful. In this process, when it takes place, the indigenous worker may be effective in serving his own psychological need to confirm his transition to a new status and a new nature, but at the same time he adds grievously to the problems of

145

his social agency in relating to its clients. He is showing in effect that the agency is so pervasively callous to its clients that even persons recently one's friends become tainted and contorted simply by joining the agency staff.

An additional limitation on the usefulness of indigenous workers in communicating between social agencies and their clients is the fact that this communication can only be as good as the program which is communicated. Although indigenous people have sometimes been used in connection with boldly innovative programs, all too often they have instead been used simply to revitalize the rather traditional policies whose many weaknesses and limited ability to benefit poor clients have already been reviewed in Chapter Four. It is questionable whether utilization of indigenous people in this way is of lasting benefit either to them or to the clients of agencies which they serve.

The self-betterment side of the argument rests upon the career implication inherent in the role of the indigenous worker. Since most of these are utilized as subprofessionals there is a promise implied in the title that they will be able to continue onward and upward in their personal development. It is in large measure from this implied future that the stature of the role derives. To move *up* from being a *subprofessional* can only mean becoming

professional. Yet in fact professional opportunities
rarely if ever exist for them. Although almost all of
the professions have demonstrated some willingness
to accept and work with aides, especially in work
with poor clients, there is nevertheless little indica-
tion that aides will ever become anything more than
just that. In order to become a certified teacher,
social worker, or psychiatrist even the most skilled
and effective aide has to go back to school (for
which he usually lacks the entering credentials) in
order to obtain the additional qualifications necessary for certification. This is a task of overwhelming
magnitude, and one for which few programs provide
adequate financial support, if indeed they provide
any. A partial exception to this has existed in the past
with respect to practical nurses. With only a high
school education and a certain amount of experience
and demonstrated ability a person could become a
licensed practical nurse, with developmental career
possibilities and clear-cut prerogatives and responsibilities, or in other words with professional status.
However, there are indications that formal require-
ments are tightening up even in this profession so
that at the very time more flexibility is needed less is
likely to be available.

For the poor person who is recruited as an indigenous worker these contradictions frequently add
up to little more than a brief glimpse of the better

life. They have an opportunity to associate on the basis of seeming equality, or at least near equality, with professional people whose work they discover depends quite as much on native intelligence and compassion as it does upon scientific knowledge. The indigenous worker therefore finds he can make a contribution truly comparable to that of his professional colleagues, and for a time he dreams of a new future full of hope and worth. Then his particular program ends and he must try to enter the job market on the basis now of his ability, not just his familiarity with a single neighborhood. He is armed with excellent letters of recommendation but no certification. At once he finds that if he is hired he will only be hired as an aide, and other programs would prefer aides from their locality. Once again he has to prove his worth since he has no piece of paper which certifies that he can be trusted. This process can go on indefinitely, but only as long as the aide is willing to expose himself to its rigors and can find programs away from "home" willing to take him in. As one rather remorseful training officer in a Community Action Agency put it, "When the poverty money runs out the indigenous worker finds he has his foot firmly planted on the bottom rung of a career ladder with only one rung."

Thus the indigenous worker strategy suffers from exactly the same dilemma which besets the larger strategies described above: any program designed to increase the social competence of poor people can only be truly successful if it can raise competence to a genuinely competitive level, or else if worthwhile careers (not just temporary jobs) are open in sufficient numbers to accommodate the graduates of programs with less ambitious goals. Although a few training projects, including rather surprisingly some for computer programmers, have had notable success in launching poor people into real careers, experience to date suggests that most graduates of short-term training can look forward only to rather modest employment prospects or, more bluntly, to second-rate jobs.

Since few of us are willing to settle for this, the answer must be sought elsewhere than in training alone. "Elsewhere" can only mean the creation of new kinds of careers, not just jobs, with training programs then being directed toward these new occupations. Whether or not these should be located in the area of personal services, as suggested above, is open to argument. But the challenge is clear for social planners and social scientists. They must think more broadly than they have in the past about the development of labor in the United States. It may well be that what seem now to be problems and deficits may in the future prove to be assets. We have before us now, as we had in the European immigrants of the past, a large pool of uncommitted and untrained manpower. Instead of wringing our hands over these people we should think more creatively about what new opportunities can be opened up, for them and for us, through capitalizing positively (rather than remedially) upon their availability.

Meanwhile, however, the discussion in this chapter should not be taken as an argument for abandoning existing job training programs. They may not help as many as we would like, and they will inevitably skim off for favor those already best prepared. Yet even at present the per capita cost is small if we remember that every person put on his feet by these programs is likely to live out his many years a productive citizen, while many of those not enrolled will for the rest of their lives be at best a drain on society, or worse its enemies. Viewed in this way we can scarcely afford not to keep on trying, and meanwhile hoping that new ways and new careers will be found to lend more value to the graduates of present as well as future programs.

7

Poverty Is Being Powerless

Ours is an affluent society. We are rich in gross national product and level of capital investment, but this does not tell all. We also enjoy the highest standard of living the world has ever known, but even this means more than merely adequate diets and high family incomes. Beyond these basic benefits unprecedented numbers of our people enjoy physical comforts that can only be classified as luxuries and have also the final luxury of being able to plan securely for themselves and ·their children. The fruits of our wealth are all about us. They present a dazzling picture which is the envy of the rest of the world.

Inevitably, however, this affluence which most of us enjoy must also be the envy of the rest of our own people who live so close to it but do not enjoy its benefits. If at one time we could comfort ourselves at least with the thought that the poor lived largely in ignorance of what life was like on our side of the tracks, assuredly television and the slick magazines have by now left no one uninformed. Indeed if anything the picture has been painted in overly opulent colors. At the same time, no matter what else has been said about the psychology of poor people, no one has seriously argued that they would not also like to enjoy the good things of life. In fact studies have repeatedly shown that poor people do consistently aspire to the American dream, a life not only with more material benefits but also with the benefits of security and opportunity for themselves and their families. Even when the realities are so overwhelming that the prospects of betterment seem completely beyond reach, poor people still desperately hope that by some means the future will be made better at least for their children if not for themselves.

It is obvious therefore that if the poor had the power to improve their lot and to obtain some of these good things they would do so. Since this does not in fact happen the conclusion that they lack the necessary power seems inescapable. Following upon this conclusion it is easy and inviting to take a further logical step and conclude that one way to improve the circumstances of the poor is to give them more actual power which they will then use to take for themselves those things which they need and which are so clearly their due. It is with the implications of this latter conclusion that we will be concerned in this chapter.

Specifically, we must seek answers to at least three questions. First, what are the forces in our society which act to render the poor powerless and to keep them that way? Second, how much power and what kind of power are required in order to assure not just tokens but the real improvements in status which true elimination of poverty implies? Finally, what are the strategies, in use or available, which can increase the real power of poor people and can these strategies be expected to deliver results, in the form of power, sufficient to make real and lasting changes in this condition we call poverty?

In seeking the forces which deny to poor people the power to change their circumstances for the better we have only to look back to the preceding three chapters. Here we dealt with the crucial characteristics of poverty: lack of money, discrimination, and lack of social and occupational skills. Each of these has a share in robbing the poor of power. Each furthermore is effective at two levels, on the one hand denying to the individual the power to determine his own destiny, and on the other draining off the impact of any collective action which numbers of poor people may jointly undertake. Let us briefly review these multiple effects.

For the individual the central fact that he lacks

money in a society in which almost every meaningful transaction involves an exchange of money severely limits his available choices and alternatives. Discrimination has the effect of defining the role of a poor person in such fashion that other people are not only inclined to make decisions affecting him without concern for his preferences or his rights, but they can also get away with acting in this cavalier fashion without fear of punishment or often even of moral criticism. Finally, the lack of social and occupational skills which so often goes with poverty restricts the ability of a poor person to chart his course through life along pathways of his choosing. In other words he lacks the material resources, the sanction, and the personal strengths necessary to convert even his minimum desires into reality.

Collectively poor people acting together are disadvantaged by these same factors quite as much as they are individually. The limitations on collective power become especially critical if one seeks to develop within the ranks of the poor themselves the impetus for social reform. Considering first the lack of money which stands at the root of poverty, it is obvious that the cumulative purchasing power of even a substantial number of poor people is small. Therefore collective withholding of purchases, even in the extreme form of a well-organized boycott, is likely to be less serious in its impact on the business community than a simple lack of enthusiasm for a product on the part of more affluent customers. Second, discrimination against a group of poor people on the basis of their ethnic or cultural identity has some of the strategic advantages suggested by the old saying about hitting the thumb with a hammer — it feels so good when you stop. Thus it often becomes easy to buy off poor people who have long suffered discrimination by offering symbolic or token concessions of little economic cost or consequence. Finally, the lack of social competence results not only in a lack of the immediate skills necessary for individual employment but also in a limited understanding on the part of most poor people of the larger world in which they live. This limited view, in turn, makes it difficult for them to devise effective strategies, such as how to deploy their collective strengths, and at what points, in order to change the system in ways that will not only be of immediate benefit to them but will also give them momentum for assaulting the barriers that lie ahead.

Since any one of these elements of poverty can seriously dilute or deflect any power toward which poor people might aspire, it is obvious that the poor must enter the competitive arena with very considerable initial force in order to surmount these and other handicaps with which they are burdened. Yet the application of this much force from any new quarter inevitably has the effect of throwing the entire system out of balance and thus bringing to bear a maximum of corrective counterforce.

Therefore we do not need to look beyond the qualities of poverty we have already reviewed in order to find an answer also to our second question. This inquires how much power would be needed to wrest from the larger society real and lasting gains for poor people. It is evident that the power required to make real changes, and to make them stick in the face of the backlash which any application of power necessarily creates, must be very considerable. Yet since the very conditions which power might be used to correct are the very same ones which undercut this power, it should be obvious that giving power to the poor is not likely by itself to prove an efficient strategy.

Furthermore, power does not build up rapidly. Having a little money and a few new social skills and a little more dignity do not yet provide an individual or a group of individuals with a substantial basis for power. When social choices are made they inevitably favor the persons with the most money, the most influence, and the greatest astuteness. Until poor people have a good deal of each of these they cannot realistically expect to originate and carry through in

competition with the existing power structure meaningful reforms in the status quo.

Thus far our discussion of the power of the poor
has been largely on a theoretical level. We must now
turn to the third question which this chapter seeks to
answer: What are the strategies which are available,
or might be available, to give to poor people the
power to work for their own betterment, and how
well can outstanding needs be met through the development of power through these means? Here,
before considering the programs and policies which
have been under trial for the past several years as
part of the official War on Poverty, mention must be
made of a more spontaneous strategy of power which
has caught the imagination of thousands, the rallying
cry of Black Power.

Almost all disadvantaged ethnic minorities including Mexican-Americans, Puerto Ricans, Indians and
Negroes have organizations dedicated to advancing
the cause of their parent groups. However, in both
structure and function Black Power stands largely
apart from organizations of this kind. In the first
place, it is an idea and a cause which transcends any
one organization, although it has been viewed hopefully as the strategic cement which could weld a
number of organizations together in concerted
action. Black Power is also widely understood to
invite Negroes to go it alone, even though on occa-

sion its proponents will argue they do not intend this at all. It commands the black man by his own power and through his own resources to wrest from a grudging white world a place of his own, a place as decent and secure and comfortable as our abundant society grants to its white citizens. Black Power is, to adapt an old phrase, a doctrine of separate but equal pathways to power and to the fruits of power. In this it departs radically from almost all other ethnic organizations, with the obvious exception of the Black Muslims. The more conventional ethnic organizations present themselves as brokers or lobbyists in the arenas of power, dedicated to obtaining for their constituents fair treatment and a fair share of the advantages our society can offer. Whether strident or modulated in their approach, these ethnic organizations have in common the premise that all the polyglot elements of the American melting pot should join hands with those in power in pursuit of the common good. They cultivate allies within this power structure and for themselves seek places in chambers of commerce and other seats of informal influence. Although their membership rules often exclude or give secondary status to outsiders, the purpose is not to go it alone but only to keep their mandate clear.

Black Power, in contrast, insists upon its blackness in order to sharpen its dialectic confrontation with whiteness. In this it goes even beyond the Black Muslims. Although Malcolm X and other Muslims have indicated their willingness to use force if necessary to maintain the separateness of black from white, their program in its day-to-day expression rests upon a peaceful policy of self-improvement which seems to be saying that, even without help from condescending whites, black people can be just as virtuous and sensible as the whites are. Black Power makes no such promises. It is not against virtue, but it has seen promises made to Negroes broken time and again and it is not going to turn the other cheek again. It is not going to make any more promises of its own until the white world delivers on some of the backlog of good works it has said would be forthcoming in return for the good deeds of black men.

Black Power is of particular relevance to us here because the good things which it hopes to command fall largely in the material realm: housing, jobs, good education, the very things which poor people of any color lack. The goals of Black Power and of the War on Poverty are virtually identical. They differ only in beneficiaries (Black Power is only for Negroes) and in strategy. Yet even with respect to beneficiaries it can be argued that if Black Power succeeds, the concept can readily be adapted to other sectors of the poor. Therefore we must ask, what are the prospects for Black Power?

Sadly, it is hard to conclude that the prospects are good. In the first place, all the inherent limitations on the power of the poor described above still apply. The power of Black Power can derive only from a mass base, and the masses of Negroes are not only almost everywhere a numerical minority in the United States, but they are also overwhelmingly poor — poor in purchasing power, poor in influence, and poor in social skills. At the same time the militancy of Black Power and the intemperance which constant disappointment has generated in some of its leaders have combined to create an image of harsh aggressiveness which accentuates the defensive reaction any movement of social reform inevitably engenders. Not only has it fueled the I-told-you-so mentality of "white backlash" and alienated much of the support of white liberals, but it has also thrown a scare into a large sector of the necessarily more conservative Negro middle class. In the long run this latter outcome may prove most disastrous of all. If there is any truth to the principle that sustained political power must rest on a solid economic base, the Black Power movement was most unwise in effectively cutting itself off from the principal economic resources within the Negro population. These resources include not only the comfortably well-off

Negro upper middle class, many of whom are already regrettably but understandably lukewarm in championing Negro rights, but also large numbers of less affluent but solid citizens reluctant to jeopardize the small security they have in pursuit of promises which, though inspiring, seem not to conform to the real world they know.

Black Power also has a secondary goal, only indirectly related to power, derived from the Populist mystique of the Student Nonviolent Coordinating Committee and its charismatic culture hero, Stokely Carmichael. This goal is to advance the thesis that it is inherently good to be black. Negroes should stand up and walk tall, commanding their rights in the name of their blackness just as whites command their privileges in the name of whiteness. It is a brave and challenging thought, appealing in its humane reasonableness — but instantly threatening to the status quo. Because of its appeal virtually all civil rights leaders have had to take some supportive posture toward it, although very few have endorsed it unequivocally. However, beyond the political imperatives of civil rights leadership virtually no other prominent Negroes have supported the cause of Black Power. Here once again is illustrated a self-defeating paradox of the Black Power concept: the very Negroes who are making their way in the world, and who presumably should provide the models for the way of life which all seek to achieve, *must* reject or ignore the Black Power slogan or else they will undermine and destroy their own hard won achievements in a world of white realities. Thus even the inspirational quality of Black Power has doubled back upon itself. Its prospects, sadly, do not look bright.

Turning now to the more conventional strategies, in one sense it could be said that since powerlessness is an almost inevitable consequence of poverty, any program designed to alleviate poverty in itself constitutes a mechanism for increasing power. Beyond this, however, the War on Poverty envisions two strategies specifically directed toward increasing the power of the poor as such. One of these is the doctrine of "maximum feasible participation of the poor" in the decision-making process in community action projects and other localized programs. Although its desirability is unquestionable this doctrine has proven very difficult to implement. A thicket of problems surrounds the determination of who should be considered proper representatives of any given group of poor people. Also, once chosen their identification with the goals of the group which they represent all too often becomes contaminated or diluted by the frequently conflicting goals of the professionals who dominate the agencies on whose boards they sit. In addition, the limited view of the world which characterizes poor people restricts their ability to design their decisions and strategies in a form which will effectively force meaningful reforms on the larger society. Their often unsophisticated understanding of social forces also makes it easy for them to be outsmarted in everything from parliamentary procedure to the drafting of truly effective policies by agencies of social reform. Finally, for poor people to exert real power through control of social agencies requires that these social agencies themselves exert enough influence on the larger community to make a real difference. Despite some early flurries over the potential threat of such pioneering programs as Mobilization for Youth, the history of anti-poverty agencies (including MFY) is not studded with accounts of major victories won in open engagements against the power structure of any community. These multiple restraints upon the power of the poor who participate in policy decisions have by now become sufficiently evident that the doctrine itself seems likely to undergo progressive modification and attrition.

The other major strategy for giving power and the instruments of power to the poor continues to have strong support in both the philosophy and programming of the War on Poverty. This strategy is most commonly referred to as community development. It consists in the organization of people in a community for mutual help and the development of democratically based systems of cooperation which can among other things increase the effectiveness of governmental and other programs.

Community development has enjoyed widespread popularity throughout the world as a device for mobilizing peasant communities which are mired in tradition and immobilized by residues of feudalism and colonialism. In these settings it has characteristically been implemented by workers with some special training and responsibility for organizing community activities. Unfortunately, experience has shown that these workers frequently become more responsive to the mandates of administrators at higher levels of government than the desires of the people they are supposed to serve. This substitution of direction from above for the local initiative which originally guides newly organized community activities is seen as a dilution of the principle of community development, but it has undoubtedly contributed mightily to the widespread popularity of this strategy, especially in the development of rural areas. It provides a ready-made device for relatively inexperienced government administrators to use in enlisting the participation of peasants in complex programs of social and economic development.

More recently the strategy of community development has been moved into the cities, both in unde-

veloped countries and in the slums of many of the
wealthier nations, including the United States.*
Urban community development characteristically
places even more emphasis than has its rural
counterpart on relationships, be they hostile or cooperative, with governmental programs. In the
United States in particular urban community development has since its beginnings placed explicit
emphasis on the development of political power
which will, among other things, enforce as well as
invite the cooperation of the government in serving
the interests of the community. A pioneer in this area
was Saul Alinsky, whose Back of the Yards movement in Chicago was the first and possibly to this
day the most successful of all such undertakings.
Much of its success undoubtedly stemmed from the
fact that it caught by surprise both city government
and the meat packing companies which dominated
the area, and wrested substantial concessions from
them, thus developing a cumulative momentum.
Further strength was derived from a large number of
European immigrants who lived in the neighborhood
who were able to provide the necessary technical
skills to man credit unions and other self-help organizations. In broad outline this pattern has been
retained, with emphasis on one feature or another,

* Marshall B. Clinard, *Slums and Community Development, Ex-
periments in Self-Help* (New York and London: Free Press, 1966).

by many of the community action projects which are now supported under the War on Poverty. Sometimes the orientation has been mainly toward power, and in other cases toward growth of more hopeful psychological attitudes and self-perceptions among the poor. The same pattern of organization has also been used under civil rights leadership in the South, with particular emphasis here upon the political objectives of voter registration and voter education among Negroes.

The urban community development programs of the War on Poverty have in general been stimulated and directed by the primarily social work staffs of the community action agencies in each city. There have been some exceptions to this direction, notably in those designed by Saul Alinsky's Industrial Areas Foundation. Although frequently drawing their funds from the same sources, the Alinsky-inspired projects often make a show of independence from competition with the more conventional anti-poverty program in the city. Particularly noteworthy was a project in Syracuse, New York, where the community development project broke away from the established community action agency and in due course developed sufficient initiative to send a petitioning group all the way to Washington to meet with the Director of the Office of Economic Opportunity.

It should be noted that regardless of the principal orientation of each, all of these community development undertakings are also intended to be effective in fostering a sense of self-worth among people in the neighborhood and particularly among those individuals who are selected to become indigenous leaders. Furthermore, insofar as cooperative activities include the provision of useful programs and services these constitute a still further gain. However, a central goal remains that of power. Through community organizations poor people will, it is hoped, for the first time find the voice to express their needs because for the first time they have not only a forum but also a mechanism through which these needs can be met and which therefore makes worthwhile the articulation of them.

How effective have these community development projects actually been in meeting the challenge they have set for themselves? This is a question which is difficult to answer conclusively even though several anti-poverty community development projects have by now accumulated two or three years of experience. Some have undoubtedly attracted attention to the problems of poor people where previously there was nothing but apathy. They have sometimes thereby led to the creation of new services, and more frequently to the modification of the programs of such key agencies as police departments. Although they have on occasion set up dramatic confrontations with the power structure, they have more often been effective in cooling off explosive situations and preventing violence and angry defiance. Whether or not this cooling off has in the long run been beneficial is debatable. But then confrontations are also debatable. Exponents of more extreme solutions contend that community action projects have degenerated into mechanisms for keeping the poor quietly in their places. However, an equally valid view is that lasting change will only come by a series of orderly and carefully designed steps which must be successively negotiated over a period of time by people in positions in power on the one hand and the representatives of the poor on the other. Thus active confrontations do not in themselves offer prima facie evidence of effective power.

In the last analysis, however, if the War on Poverty is truly intended to cure the causes of poverty and not merely to relieve some of its symptoms, the power of the poor fostered by its programs can be judged sufficient only if it is able to generate major, meaningful and lasting social and economic reforms in conformity with the expressed wishes of poor people. Although this is admittedly a heavy requirement to place upon any program, it is in reality the only criterion which can properly be applied in judgment of the community development activities under the War on Poverty if we are to take seriously its stated objectives. If we adopt this standard it is extremely difficult to find even scattered evidence of success. Instead one perhaps finds health services a little more available, policemen a bit easier to get along with, sometimes a considerable increase in recreation facilities. But the poor remain as poor as ever, and the "power structure" remains the place where the power actually lies. Compared to the needs for reform which are essential if permanent solutions are to be found for poverty as we know it in the 1960's, the concessions which have been wrung from the power structure in virtually all communities are so trifling as to be almost inconsequential. In all honesty it is therefore hard to claim the strategy of community development as applied under the War on Poverty in American cities has made good on its promise of giving the poor power to effect the changes necessary for their lasting rehabilitation.

What are the reasons for this failure? A number of these have already been mentioned. As we saw earlier in this chapter the very nature of the life of poverty is such that any development of power at the grass roots level is difficult if not impossible of achievement. The poverty programs have to some degree themselves recognized these obstacles which lie in the path of efforts simply to develop naked power alone. They have instead designed multiple-pronged programs which include not only political mobilization for power, but also skill training, community relations programs designed to reduce discrimination, and other activities designed to touch upon the various facets of poverty. However, it has proven extremely difficult to bring even these more flexible tactics to bear simultaneously and in concert. Thus skill training is often concentrated principally at the adolescent level whereas political development goes forward among people of voting age, and defiant political statements from one quarter disrupt the harmony necessary to the success of attempts elsewhere to reduce discrimination. Consequently power-oriented programs frequently undercut the companion activities designed in part to strengthen the base of this power.

However, most important of all is the question of whether it is possible in our society for any disadvantaged minority group, economic or ethnic, through its own efforts to achieve reforms which will serve principally its own interests. The civil rights movement seemed at first to answer this question in the affirmative. Major legislation was enacted in response to grass roots activities by Negroes, including many who were poor. However, the issue at stake was one of compelling moral force and one which was intimately intertwined with the very reasons for which the United States came into being as an independent nation. Furthermore, although the legislation enacted in the name of civil rights has had important effects on the customs and institutions of the country, it can be argued that its net effect was only to give substance to principles already clearly enunciated in the Constitution of the United States and in the Christian ethic upon which it was founded.

The War on Poverty is very different in the demands it makes, and its moral mandate is far more ambiguous. At the same time the elimination of poverty as this is currently understood requires major changes in business practices and in the way power is controlled and wielded, changes which are bound in turn to generate both fear and stubborn resistance. In an earlier chapter we noted that in designing the programs of the New Deal in the 1930's an assumption was made that the power to effect major structural reforms could only come from above, that is, from the Federal Government. The War on Poverty has rejected this strategy and has instead taken the position that reforms must come from the poor themselves. From this it follows that one of the functions of poverty-inspired programs is to aid the poor in developing the wisdom and the power to implement such reforms with community development a principal pathway toward this goal. The question can still be considered open whether the lack thus far of major alterations in the social and economic fabric of the nation really means that major reforms are not possible when they start from the grass roots and affect only a small proportion of the population. However, as time passes by and reforms are still out of reach, the basic premises of community development as a strategy of power and therefore of reform become increasingly suspect.

8

Evolution, Revolution, or Disaster?

THE TROOPS are marching and countermarching, the dust of battle rises above the plain. How goes the War on Poverty? As far as the eye can see, no commanding heights have yet been captured, and the casualty lists have sometimes been long. Can we yet win the war?

The long hot summers keep getting longer and hotter. The sparks of discontent seem still to burst most readily into flame in the Negro ghettos of our cities, but the big riots in Chicago in the summer of 1966 began in a Puerto Rican area, underscoring the fact that although ghettos contain only poor people, not all of them are black. Yet the "white backlash," regardless of its intended target, is having its political and human impact on poor people generally. Segregationists tend to view the poverty program as nothing more than a thinly veiled effort to further promote the Negro cause. Meanwhile, there is very little evidence that the poor are really getting any richer, that families bedeviled by poverty are becoming any more stable, or that the power for reform has moved away from its traditional locus in the white middle-class establishment.

Yet things have changed, whether for better or for worse. The machinery we have devised thus far to dispose of the waste of poverty and raise the poor to self-sufficiency may not be working very well, but it has at least raised the pressure in the boiler. Hope has been given to the hopeless — but then alas too often taken away again, leaving anger behind. The future is far from clear. What had been planned as an orderly evolution, a gradual opening up of opportunity and power for those now poor and powerless, may yet take a more revolutionary turn with more violence, more hatred and more backlash. Or repeated disappointment and disillusionment may lead finally to resignation, bitter but quiet, while a new set of laws and practices evolve to assure that things do not "get out of hand" again. Thus the War on Poverty could end as the Reconstruction did scarcely a century ago with some of the rules changed and a few people better off than they were before, but the same old game being played with the same winners and the same losers. In the long run the second outcome is probably even sadder to contemplate than the first. Are these pessimistic prospects the only ones we can envision?

They have deeply concerned a lot of people, including a number of social scientists. It is very proper that social scientists should be concerned because the basic premises of the War on Poverty were largely developed by them. The theories of poverty, the pilot projects, even the books on the shelves of the poverty warriors bear the stamp of social science. Every major strategy of the War on Poverty finds not only its protagonists but often its architects among the ranks of social scientists. They cannot be held responsible for all the mistakes that may have been made. But they must accept a good deal of blame for advice which has had a good test and has been found wanting.*

Yet no one else seems to be coming forward with alternative suggestions. So with humility we must look at the experience thus far, see what we have learned, and consider alternative strategies which might be more realistic and more effective in the future. It may be too late. Perhaps no one is listening any more, but still we have an obligation to see

* The present writer is no exception. See his "The Anthropologist's View of Poverty," in *Social Welfare Forum 1961* of the National Conference on Social Welfare (New York: Columbia University Press, 1961, pp. 73–86), in which he came out strongly for community development.

where things went wrong and what can be done better. This book has been an attempt in this direction. What, then, have we learned?

A central strategic assumption of the War on Poverty has been that both the causes and the solutions to the problems of poverty are to be found largely within the ranks of the unskilled, unorganized and disheartened poor. Thus, given skills they will advance themselves and open the door to opportunity; given organization they will grow in power and bring about social reforms; and given hope they will grow in both dignity and responsibility. Although this set of assumptions arises directly from the fashionable and plausible concept of a culture of poverty, it ignores much of what we have learned from sociologists, economists and political scientists about the way large masses of money and power within our society can effectively determine the choices open to people at any level in the social structure. Therefore, if there is a central argument to this book it is that the social reforms necessary to make poverty avoidable and remediable must embrace a larger part of our society than just the poor alone, and that these reforms can be implemented only by forces greater than those conceivably available to poor people, however well organized. These reforms must furthermore reallocate power, and above all money and the power that flows from

money, within our society or else the poor will remain forever poor.

We are not without precedents for such a program
of reform. We have before us the history of the New
Deal. Its scope and strategies were discussed in
Chapter Two. In the 1930's major changes in social
and economic systems were possible because of an
almost universal realization that the society as a
whole was sick, and that the economic rules by
which it had been governed were no longer working.
Once the need for basic change was recognized the
only question was the form it should take.

But the American society of the 1960's does not
find itself impelled toward change. Domestically at
least the majority of the voters appear satisfied, and
in fact many complain that they have already seen
too many changes in a way of life which *they* find
uniquely comfortable. Yet our society is sick, potentially as sick as it was in the 1930's. At present we see
the acute symptoms of its illness only in the distress
of urban ghettos, the destitution of backwaters like
Appalachia, and the wastage of uneducated children.
But in the long run greater wastage and even more
widespread disorganization lies close ahead. We do
not lack for prophets of this future, telling us of the
cybernetic revolution, technological unemployment,
and the perils of leisure. The work without which we
believe a man's life has no dignity or meaning is, we

are told, gradually being whittled away from all of us, not just from the presently poor. What will take its place? We have no plans, nor even studies of what is to come — only projections forward of what has been and is now. All we know is that sooner or later, even if the current unrest of the very poor sputters out and becomes quiet, a new sickness will inevitably overtake larger and larger sectors of our labor force, which of course means larger sectors of our total population. Then we will once again be forced to make the kind of real reforms which the New Deal made. The need in this case will perhaps be to correct not so much unemployment as disorganized and unsatisfying employment, yet the sickness will be as real. Poverty and its symptoms are thus signs and warnings of more trouble which lies in the future. They tell us we must start thinking ever harder about our social problems and looking harder for solutions, both present and future.

The reforms which have been suggested in this book fall broadly at two levels. First there are those designed to attack the immediate causes of poverty. They would put a floor under deprivation, a resilient floor such that persons who fall into adversity and become really poor will be able to bounce back on their feet and reach upward again toward opportunity. The strategies here include a guaranteed income sufficient to assure at least the minimum of

178

decency and security without which normal family functioning and psychological stability are impossible. Related to this, major reforms in welfare have been proposed. With a guaranteed income fulfilling the sustaining function of traditional welfare programs, a new welfare can be built on a strategy of enablement, giving poor people the same kind of resources for self-help and self-improvement which the original GI Bill gave our veterans of World War II. Included also in the strategies specific to poverty are educational reforms which can assure that while parents are struggling to surmount their own distress their children do not meanwhile fall victim to the same handicaps. Education is a complex and difficult field in which there are many problems yet to be solved and battles to be won, but it is one which has been addressed squarely and often creatively by social and educational reformers, even though institutional change in school systems is sometimes agonizingly slow.

Yet we must realize there are real limitations to what can be accomplished by strictly anti-poverty measures, at best only remedial or preventive. They can do no more than keep people with the misfortune to be really poor from being locked in a chain of circumstances which keeps them so forever. True, much of this book has been devoted to an analysis of these circumstances and their multiple and interlocking effects. Lack of money, lack of opportunity and lack of skill all conspire to assure that once a person becomes sufficiently poor his chances of ever rising again become very small. These are the factors which make the condition of poverty seem hopeless. Yet even if the strategies here proposed or endorsed should prove effective in breaking the cycle of extreme poverty whenever it appears, this is no more than an interim level of reform.

The anti-poverty interventions can accomplish only temporary gains if more basic reforms are not made in the structure of opportunity and the utilization of human resources in our nation as a whole. It is by now clear that expanding opportunities can no longer be sought in traditional areas of occupational advancement. It has been proposed here, certainly not for the first time, that the essentially interpersonal occupations which constitute the service area of employment are the ones which must provide new opportunities for the future. This is true not only for people who are poor but also for an ever growing proportion of our entire labor force. It is therefore urgent to our total welfare that service employment become an immediate subject of study. Creative solutions must be found for the many problems which presently beset the process of recruitment and training of workers and the purchase and delivery of services. As we look at patterns of service employment and labor utilization it is obvious that they are characterized by a multitude of illogical attitudes and practices which are at best haphazard and sometimes border upon the irrational. Planning and the development of new ideas must therefore go forward quite as strongly in the psychological domain as in the economic and social. This is compatible with the already rapidly growing role of psychology in more traditional economic spheres, as in market research, public relations, concern with corporate image, or product appeal. Yet all these deal with things, and particularly with manufacturing and selling things. The essence, then, of the second strategy of reform is the application to *people* and to the production and marketing of personal services of the psychological understandings and research techniques which are already coming into vogue for marketing *things*.

The War on Poverty and its antecedents in civil rights have given us a concern both compassionate and practical with human beings and their plight. We have quite properly pitied poor people their helplessness as they struggle with a system which baffles them at every turn and strips them not only of security but of dignity and meaning for their lives. The effort to conquer poverty has thus far been a purifying even if not always a successful experience. But if there is a larger message to be learned from this experience it is that the bafflement of the poor today is only a harbinger of the greater distress which lies just beyond the next bend in the road. It will beset us all if we do not see poverty now for what it really is, a loose strand in the gradually unraveling fabric of our whole society. This is the true moral of the story of poverty. It is one none of us can afford to disregard.